A Better Life with Your Dog

Understanding and Improving
the Way You and Your Dog Live Together

Fernando Camacho

Photographs taken by John McGall
www.dirtydogphotography.com

First published by Dog Ear Publishing
4010 W. 86th Street, Ste H
Indianapolis, IN 46268
www.dogearpublishing.net

dog Near
PUBLISHING

ISBN: 978-160844-277-5

This paper is acid free and meets all ANSI standards for archival
quality paper.
Printed in the United States of America

For my three girls: Sabrina, Jada and Hayley.

Table of Contents

Acknowledgments

I'm a lucky guy. Not only do I get to spend my days helping dogs and people live together better, but I also have the opportunity to throw my thoughts down in a book and have you believe in me enough to spend your hard-earned money on it. So since this is the section where I'm supposed to thank the people that made this book possible, I feel it necessary to start with you. Thanks for caring about your dog and looking for better ways to educate yourself on how you can make your relationship with your dog better and stronger.

I'm also very lucky to have the greatest wife on the planet. Michele has the amazing ability to listen to all of my ideas without bursting into laughter, to endure my many dog anecdotes without yawning, and to giggle at my jokes when they're not funny (most of the time). All of my successes in life are a direct result of her support and encouragement.

I'm very proud to be where I am in my career, but realize that I did not get here on my own. I've been blessed to have some wonderful people in my life that really believe in me and continue to go out of their way to help me further my career with dogs. Jeff Coltenback is one such person. Jeff's the guy who gave me the first push to pursue a career in dog training and gladly makes himself available whenever I need assistance or guidance.

I also need to thank Liz Bratman, owner of Rover Ranch and Spa, who gave me the opportunity to work in a dog pack and learn all about the canine world. She is always supportive of everything I do, and continues to be a driving force behind my success.

Next on my list is Ken Brower of Four Paws Stay and Play, another great doggie daycare in New Jersey. Ken and I met just as I began my journey with dogs, and we immediately hit it off. We knew right away that we were incredibly likeminded when it came to dog care, and made a pact to work together to help people and their dogs. In addition to their endless encouragement, both Liz and Ken generously allow me to hijack their facilities for any event, seminar, or class.

Turning my thoughts, ideas and rants into something cohesive and grammatically appropriate was no easy task. Luckily, I had Meagan DeJong and Leslie Robinson in my corner to edit the many grammatical liberties I took, as well as make sense of my sometimes incoherent ramblings. To enhance the visual component of this book, I was fortunate enough to aquire the expert photographic skills of John McGall of Dirty Dog Photography, who was gracious enough to take all the pictures in and on this book.

Lastly, I am forever indebted to every single dog that I've had the pleasure to work with. I truly believe that life is not full unless there's a dog lounging at your feet, sitting on your lap, or even perched on your head. It's such a thrill to see firsthand how dogs impact the lives of the human families they live with. So I thank all the dogs out there for putting up with all of our human nonsense and teaching us how to really live.

Introduction

If you opened this book you're probably asking yourself the big question: "Who the hell is this 'Fern' guy and why should I listen to a word he says about dogs?" Well, it might be easier if I start off by telling you who I am not. I am not a scientist. I haven't spent years in a controlled clinical setting going over detailed data. I don't have a large vocabulary of scientific terms and conditions. And I don't have charts of any kind: pie, bar or otherwise. I am not a veterinarian. I do not have any diplomas hanging on my wall. I don't own a white lab coat. And I have never stuck my finger up any animal's butt.

I am also not an expert. Mostly because I really don't believe that anyone can really be an expert in dog behavior. In my opinion, the only experts are dogs themselves. No matter how much we may think we know about them, or any animal species, we are still only speculating and making assumptions.

So now that we've covered what I'm not, let's go over what I am. Basically, I'm a guy with a dog. In addition to that, I'm a dog be-havior consultant and trainer, but mostly I'm just a guy with a dog. I wrote this book to help other guys and gals with dogs get more out of their day-to-day life with their furry pals. It doesn't matter if your dog acts like Marley or Lassie; there are things you can do right now to improve your life together, insuring that you will all live happily ever after.

I first decided to become a behavior consultant/trainer because I have a great relationship with my dog, and started to notice that not everyone was having the same experience. It's hard to take pleasure in the everyday joys of having a dog when you're being dragged down the street, looking down the hole that was just dug in your carpet, or being serenaded by yet another hour of barking. All that stuff tends to taint even the calm, quite times with your pooch.

If you have one of these dogs that seems to make you crazy more than happy, take comfort in the fact that it doesn't have to be that way. You can have a better dog, and a better life with your dog – it just takes a little knowledge. The big problem is that most of us take for granted what it takes to own a dog. We get a dog and just assume we know how to raise a good puppy and train a good dog. In reality, we can only do the best with the information we have at hand. And most of us are not educated enough to help our dog develop into a well-adjusted dog in this very human world.

It really surprises me that so many people put such little thought into getting a dog, and what it takes to keep both dog and owner living happily together. Too many of us jump into the emotional aspect of having a dog that we forget that we may not have the proper knowledge or environment to handle it. You must have an open mind to accept the fact that you might not know the best way to train your dog, and then take steps to educate yourself as much as possible, and never stop learning. If you have problems with your dog and you do nothing, guess what? Nothing will change. Odds are, the problems will only escalate and make treating them more difficult and time consuming. Don't sit idle and hope annoying behaviors will just go away on their own. Your dog is telling you that whatever you're doing isn't working, so listen to him and find out what you need to do to solve the issues.

That is what I hope this book will do for you. Give you some information to fill up your toolbox and empower you with knowledge - and as far as knowledge is concerned, the more the better. There are about a-gazillion books out there on dog behavior and training, so allow me answer another big question that's sure to be on your mind, "Is this book different than the rest?" The answer is not really . . . and very.

I've read a large variety of books on dog behavior, but found most of them were not really designed for the average guy with a dog. They are all very well researched and have lots of dog training buzz words like "operant conditioning" and "positive punishment," and cite studies done by people like B.F. Skinner and Ivan Pavlov, but seem a bit too much for the average person who just wants a better behaved dog. Most are packed with information, but are not easy or fun to read. So for those of you who are not as concerned with the statistics and science behind it all, but still need a balanced and happy pooch, this book is for you.

Once you apply the suggestions contained in this book and see the results in your new and improved dog, you may be so fired up that you'll want to learn more and discover the specifics and research that has led dog behaviorists and trainers to where they are today. Then you can go out and read more. Educate yourself as much as you can and learn from everyone, no matter what their style or perspective. When I decided to make dogs my career I spoke to any and every trainer that would put up with me. Even if I didn't agree with their methods or training philosophy, I still came away with new knowledge. I strongly believe that having an open mind is a crucial element in every aspect of life, dog training included. Take bits and pieces from every book, trainer, dog owner and relative that throws advice your way, edit out the nonsense, and combine it all to create your own individual method of training your dog. I've met many dog professionals who are so hung up on their way of training that they automatically discount anything contrary. That's a big mistake, because as we now know, there are no "experts" in the field. Every person is different, and so is every dog. So keep an open mind and always be willing to entertain new ideas.

There are many great dog professionals that have influenced and aided me as I continue my career with dogs. Some names you've heard of, and others are unknown except to the people and dogs they've helped. What's interesting about many of the trainers that I learned techniques from is that their training styles are often complete opposites of one another. Yet I draw upon methods from all of them, mixing them together to create my own unique style of training. Ahhhh, the beauty of an open mind.

With all of these great dog trainers out there, it's hard to believe that I could find a better source to help me understand dogs, and to teach me how to work with them, but I did. I was fortunate enough to have an opportunity to study with the best minds available on the subject of dog behavior; those who are at the very forefront of all things canine. The true - dare I say – experts in the field. Oh yes indeed, you guessed it, I'm talking about a pack of dogs, baby!

I knew from the beginning that they were the ones that would teach me what I needed to know. They were the ones to instruct me how to communicate on a canine level. They were the ones that would show me how dogs stayed happy and healthy in the human world. And, occasionally, they were also the ones that would pee on my feet.

I've worked with many great trainers, read countless books, and attended lots of seminars, but nothing has come close to the education I received by standing among a pack of dogs every day. The moment I decided to make dogs my career, I walked into a doggie daycare, and accepted a job watching the daily packs. The pay wasn't great, and the smell at times was less than fragrant, but the benefits were immeasurable.

I credit them for anything and everything I do with dogs. And that's my perspective on living with dogs. I try to think like them in order to understand and treat the conflicts that arise when dogs live in the human world. They've done their part and abandoned their wild ways of life to join us in a very unfamiliar environment, and now it's up to us to do everything we can to make it a happy and healthy life for them. So I invite you to open your mind, put away your human side, enter the canine world, and begin to think like a dog (butt sniffing optional).

1

Ask Not What
Your Dog Can Do For You . . .

My wife loves to ask couples who have been married for a long time what their secret is to staying to together while so many others split up. Although most of the answers are typical "Hallmark" stuff, every once in a while she gets a memorable nugget (including one woman who said the key to staying together was spending lots of time apart – my wife wasn't too happy with that one). One couple who had been married for twenty-six years told us the reason why they have outlasted so many other relationships is that they always put their partner's needs first, no matter what.

I think there's a lot of wisdom in that little piece of advice. Always put your partner's needs above and before yours. By doing that, you are ensuring that you will have a happy spouse for years to come. That makes good sense in any relationship you have, especially the one with your dog. By taking care of your dog's needs before yours, you are setting the stage for a long and happy life with him.

Dogs are happy to accept our invitation to join us in the human world but that doesn't change the fact that they are, and always will be, dogs. Yes, even that little Chihuahua dressed in designer clothes, wearing more bling-bling than Mr. T is still a typical dog. I don't care if you refer to him as your "widdle baby" or carry him around in a custom backpack, or if he sits at the table and eats dinner with you, he's still a dog – with all the needs of a dog.

I know this may come as a shock to some of you out there and I'm sorry to say something so utterly controversial so early in the book, but I feel obligated to inform you of this cold hard truth: your dog is a dog.

In my opinion, the biggest injustice you can do to your dog is to treat him like a furry person. He is a proud member of the canine family and deserves to be treated like one. Now, before all you bling-bling Chihuahua owners start getting upset that I'm about to take away all of the fun you have with your dog, let me offer two short pieces of advice. One, never use Paris Hilton as a model for dog ownership; and two, you can still dress up your dog, and tuck him in at night (as I do), and spoil him rotten – but only after all of his basic canine needs are fulfilled. Because although you will swear to me that he just loves wearing his Juicy Couture Sweat Suit, and needs to be wheeled through the park in the dog version of the Popemobile, I'm here to tell you that those actions are only satisfying your needs, not his.

The big concept you need to understand is that you can do all of that stuff with your dog, but never before you take care of what he needs first. Once all his needs are fulfilled, he will be more than happy to indulge you in the things that make you happy. If all of your dog's needs are not properly met, you'll know it. You'll know it because he'll let you know very clearly. He'll tell you by using your house like a pinball machine where he's the ball. He'll tell you by barking at anything and everything. And he'll tell you by not responding to any of your instructions, yells or pleas.

All behavior problems in dogs are really just their way of saying that they are not fulfilled in some way. Something is missing in their life and they are letting us know. So now is the time we stop making excuses by saying things like, "he's still a puppy" or "it's because of his breed" or any of the other cop-outs that we humans come up with in order to avoid the truth: we are the reasons our dogs are misbehaving. Most of the time, it's not because of something we're doing, it's because of the things we're not doing.

So let's get down to it. What are the basic canine needs of our dogs? You probably already know what they are, but you are either not executing them properly or have neglected them completely. However, it's never too late to help your dog and change your life with him. It all starts with an open mind and the power of becoming informed.

Basic Canine Need #1: Leadership

Basic Canine Need #2: Exercise

Basic Canine Need #3: Adequate Walks

Basic Canine Need #4: Proper Nutrition

There are other secondary needs, but these are big four that are non-negotiable. If each of these needs are not met, your dog will not be living a full, happy life and you will more than likely feel the effects of his discontent. Now, I'm not saying that by taking care of all four of these that your dog will magically stop jumping up on people. But fulfilling these needs can make everything you do with your dog easier. Training, communication, and pretty much any interaction you or anyone else has with your dog will improve.

I'm sure that no one is surprised by this list, but you need to ask yourself if you are doing everything in your power to fulfill these needs for your dog. Keep in mind that every dog is an individual and will have a different ratio of which needs require more attention, but all dogs, no matter what age, breed, or personality, need these four items checked off every single day. And remember, what you think is adequate leadership, exercise, walking and nutrition may be way off from what your dog actually requires.

Of course, I realize that our human world comes with a slew of responsibilities and demands that can make it a challenge to find the time, money and energy to adequately fulfill all of these needs. However, we can certainly make more of an effort. I think you'll be surprised at what can be accomplished with a little determination and prioritizing. Think back to the day that you decided to invite your dog into your life. You probably told yourself that you would be a good owner and take good care of your new dog. Maybe you started out strong, but then got a little busy or lazy or never really looked into what it takes to properly take care of your new furry family member. No matter what your story is, don't dwell on the mistakes of the past. Concentrate on making a better future for you and your dog, starting right now.

It's time to really be honest and ask ourselves: are we really doing all we can to satisfy the needs of our dogs? If the answer is no, then now is the time to take some action to change ourselves and improve the lives of our dogs, thereby enhancing our relationships with them. I'll go over each of these basic canine needs in detail in later chapters, as well as offer some options and examples, depending on your individual dog and lifestyle.

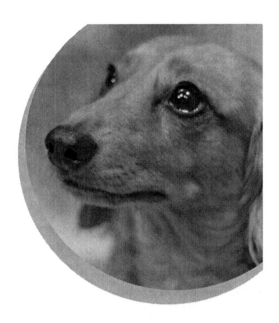

2 Conserve Energy

All living things give off a certain kind of energy and can be influenced by the energy around them. You, sitting there reading this book are giving off energy and can easily be affected by someone else's energy when that person enters the same space.

Is this notion a little too "new age" for some of you? Not sold on this concept of energy yet? Well, let me give you a few examples to help you understand the concept of energy, and what it means to us and our dogs. Have you ever walked into a room where two people were just having a heated argument? They both get quiet upon your arrival, but you can still feel the tension in the air. That's energy. Their argument may have temporarily ceased but the energy that they are creating in the room is unmistakable.

Do you have any friends that just seem to have fun all the time? They are always doing fun things, have oodles of great stories and are just plain fun to be around. They are the life of the party, and things seem to get much more interesting when they enter a room. Their happy, positive energy immediately influences your mood and outlook. That's energy in action.

I hope we can all agree that energy is a very real thing and understand the powerful effect that energy can have on others. This is especially true of our doggie companions, and if we're not careful, their energy can grab us and take us for a wild ride. However, with a little awareness and practice, our energy can prevail and greatly influence our dogs.

In a pack of dogs it is amazing to observe how one dog's energy can impact the entire group. Just watch as a six-month old Boxer puppy enters the dog park. As soon as he's off leash he'll run head-on into the other dogs, bounding and leaping just before taking off at warp speed to do a few laps around the perimeter of the park. That one dog will have the whole pack in an uproar in seconds. Soon, most of the dogs have given chase or are yelping as he zips by. Even that lethargic old lab breaks into a rarely seen trot.

Since most of our dogs greatly lack exercise (we'll get into that later), they tend to have a pretty high energy level most of the time, making your primary goal controlling that energy as much as possible. And the first line of defense is your own energy. Whenever you want to communicate anything to your dog you must be in a calm state of mind in order to properly influence him. The more I'm around dogs, the more I realize just how important and powerful calm energy is.

I want you to picture your dog as the Tasmanian Devil of Bugs Bunny cartoon fame. If you remember, whenever Taz got worked up, his image would become a mass of limbs in a tornado. Sound familiar? It should, because that's probably what your dog looks like when he's running around the house getting into all kinds of trouble. If we're not careful, that whirlwind of manic energy can suck us in, and before we know it we're chasing him around, arms flailing, yelling at the top of our lungs - now surely, that sounds familiar. Your dog's excited energy prevailed over yours, and now your frenzied display has added to the energy in the room, making it bigger, more powerful, and more difficult to defuse. Allowing your dog to get you worked up is basically equivalent to throwing gasoline on a fire.

However, if you can stay calm amidst the chaos, your energy can bring your dog down from his energy rush. This sounds simple but it can be pretty challenging at first. It will take a lot of conscious effort on your part to stay calm as your dog is causing so much havoc around you. It takes practice, but can be accomplished. I once had a client with a Cockapoo puppy that was driving her crazy by constantly running around her feet and biting at her clothes (all you Cockapoo owners surely feel her pain). As her little dog ran circles around her with a decent-sized strip of her shirt between his teeth, she chased him and shouted at him, using some choice words that I dare not repeat here. After removing her from the room and talking her down from her heightened state of frustration, I entered the room with the puppy and was met with the same boisterous greeting. However, instead of immediately reacting to his antics, I simply crouched down resting my elbows on my knees, with my hands open in front of me. The little pup, sparked by my getting closer, darted back and forth, taking generous nips at my fingers. I remained calm and motionless, looking down at the pup with soft eyes. Within thirty seconds he was standing in front of me, looking up, wondering how I could be so unaffected by all the fun he was having.

Now, he's a puppy – a Cockapoo puppy – so it doesn't take much to get him going again, but if you continually stay calm you will affect your dog's energy over the long term. You need to be a calming influence to your dog instead of a trigger for excitement. That's why I like to break up play every once in a while, get the dog back to a calm state of mind then let him go play again. It gives you the power to take your dog from a high level of arousal back down to zero.

When I worked at the doggie daycare I would constantly break up play. I would interrupt the dogs, make eye contact with them, and wait until they returned to a calm state of mind. Then I would say "go play" and let them get revved up again. By doing this repeatedly, I became a calming influence whenever I entered their space. This also made it easy for me to intervene during altercations between dogs, since they were so used to me breaking them up during normal play.

Calm energy is the key to all communication with your dog. Nothing will ever get across to your dog when you're running and screaming at him. It's pretty simple really, either you are going to be affected by his energy or he will be influenced by yours.

Mind Power

Just as it's important for you to be in a calm state of mind, it's also vital to make sure that easily excitable dog of yours shares your mindset. Dogs are lovers of life and it usually doesn't take much to get them all charged up and in a frenzy. The key to having a well-behaved dog is to consistently guide his state of mind from excited to calm.

This requires some patience and consistency on your part. The big thing to remember here is that whenever your dog receives any kind of reward (as seen by him – which could be different from what you consider a reward) you are reinforcing whatever he's doing at that exact moment, as well as his state of mind at that moment. Let's go out on a limb here and say your dog loves food and gets a little fired up when he sees that his next meal is being prepared. Now let's assume you're a good, responsible dog owner and require a little show of manners from your dog before he inhales his food. Maybe you have him sit and then let him know when his chow time can officially begin. Now, if he sits there gazing down at the bowl like a love-crazed teenager, while his whole body twitches in anticipation and you release him to attack his food, what state of mind are you rewarding? You guessed it, an excited one. Sure he sat as he was told to, but by rewarding this state of mind you are continually fortifying the cycle of mealtime craziness.

His state of mind is more important than his actions at that time. In this scenario, what you need to do is have him sit and then wait until the excitement passes and you have a nice calm dog again. Then, and only then, should you release and reward him. How long you have to wait depends on the dog, but if it takes ten minutes for him to calm down, then get comfy and wait. If you repeatedly reward an excited mind, then an excited mind is what you'll get more often than not. However, if your dog is only rewarded in a calm state of mind, then that will become his default mindset. Once he figures out that all the good things in life only happen when he's calm, he will abandon the excited behavior (or at least calm down quickly) because that's always the short cut to what he wants. Sometimes, we get so focused on what the dog is doing that we overlook the state of mind he's in.

This is especially important if you have a dog with any kind of fear or anxiety. What typically happens is that the dog has what he perceives to be a negative experience with a certain stimulus, and becomes fearful or anxious. It's important to remember that you may not see what the dog is reacting to as traumatic, but it's not about you. It's what the dog perceives as a negative or scary experience - it could be something as trivial as an object falling off of the table.

To help your dog avoid picking up any fears or phobias, it is absolutely essential that you never give any kind of affection to a fearful or anxious mind. Remember, whenever you give affection you are reinforcing that state of mind in that situation. A typical example is thunder. Thunder booms overhead and your dog is startled by it, shakes and runs over and leans close to you. If you do what human nature tells you to do and soothe the dog, saying "It's OK boy, don't be scared" as you gently pet him, you are guaranteeing that he will go right back into that state of mind the next time he hears thunder. He associates the trigger (the thunder) with his state of mind when he received affection, which was fear. If you ignore the dog in that situation and go about your business like nothing's wrong (because there is nothing wrong and nothing to be afraid of) then your dog will take his cue from you and get over it.

That works great for new situations, but what if your dog already has a fearful or anxious association? Well, in this situation, you need to work on the circumstances that cause the reaction, but at a low level of intensity or at a distance where the dog is showing a reaction but not totally freaking out or shutting down. You then work with the dog – no matter how long it takes – to get them back to a calm, more relaxed state of mind. It might be as simple as letting the dog react but doing nothing and waiting. Let him go through his typical routine around the stimulus and release the energy that comes with it. Then, when he realizes that nothing bad has happened to him, he should start to show signs of adjustment.

To be successful you must control the environment as completely as possible. If you're trying to help your dog overcome fear or aggression toward other dogs, you will have to set up situations with dogs and handlers you know. That way, you can have them stand still or move depending on the dog's needs. It's very difficult to try to address this kind of issue on your own, because on a walk with your dog you never know what kind of dogs you will encounter. And you probably can't tell the people walking them to hang out while you spend the needed time to transform your dog's state of mind. Also, you must not allow your dog to have an experience that reinforces his fearful or aggressive mindset, which once again, is very difficult because you never know what you're going to encounter on an average walk.

When working with any kind of fear or anxiety issue remember that it's never a quick fix. It takes time and patience to help a dog that may have had a experienced that unstable frame of mind on numerous occasions. That's why it's so important to address these problems very early on when they first present themselves. Too many people just ignore it and hope it will magically get better.

Always be very aware of your dog's state of mind at all times, make sure you're not inadvertently rewarding an unbalanced mind, and address any concerns as soon as they present themselves. If you take the time to work with your dog and help him achieve a nice calm state of mind in a variety of circumstances and among varying stimuli, you will be creating a better, calmer dog overall.

3 Take Me To Your Leader

Leadership, as it applies to our dogs, is a subject that is often talked about but rarely fully understood. Many people throw the word around (along with the word "dominance") without really taking the time to figure out exactly what it means, and how to apply it to our daily lives with our dogs. I've seen many uninformed dog owners do some really unnecessary and inhumane things in the name of leadership. Leadership is a very important part of a dog's life and is one of his basic canine needs, but it must be done the right way.

The secret of leadership starts with a dog pack. Dogs form packs for survival purposes, in which each dog depends on the others in the group and together make up a well-organized unit. It's set up similarly to the United States Military. Each dog holds a specific and very publicly known rank, and will only take orders from those that hold a higher rank. At the top is the alpha dog, or general, and at the bottom of the chain of command is the omega dog, or private. Unlike the U.S. Military though, a dog pack has two parallel hierarchies: one male and one female. So there's an alpha male and alpha female, and dogs of the opposite sex will never compete for the same position in the pack.

That's why, if you're planning on adding a second dog to your household, you should pick the opposite sex of the dog you already have. This way, you won't have any power struggles over rank, unless it comes down to only one resource available, for example, they both find one bone. Then there will be a determination as to who the boss is and who gets the booty. That's not to say that if you have a male dog and get a female there won't be problems, it just means that at least they won't fight over status. It also doesn't mean that if you have two same-sex dogs that there's automatically going to be trouble. It all depends on the individual dogs themselves.

In the domestic setting, the pack includes everyone in the household, including cats and human babies. I once had a client with a cat and two German Shepherds and guess who ran the show? Would you believe the cat was in the top spot? I wouldn't have believed it if I hadn't seen it with my own eyes, but those two big dogs would always defer to the cat, which strutted around the house like a king.

This example proves that size is not a factor in deciding who will be the leader. Just because you're bigger than your dog don't assume for a second that you hold the top spot in your dog's eyes. I've seen tiny little Yorkies boss around one hundred pound Labs. So, if it's not size that matters, how do those little guys gain leadership over those giant breeds and us tall humans?

If I asked you to tell me who you thought was the alpha dog at the dog park, most people would probably guess wrong. It's not the dog that's constantly mounting the other dogs, or the one that's barking and yelping at everyone, and it's not that dog that picks on the shy dog in the corner for no apparent reason. It's the dog you don't notice - the dog that walks into the dog park with his tail held high and just allows everyone to come over and sniff him. He moves effortlessly through the pack, as all the other dogs part the way to let him pass. It's the dog that doesn't have to "tell" the pack that he's the top dog, they all just instinctively know.

How does he do it? It's all a matter of body language and confidence. The main form of dog communication is body language. Dogs are masters of perceiving body positions and postures, enabling them to speak in great detail to one another without a sound. They use every inch of their bodies to convey what's on their mind.

That's where leadership begins for us: body language. Your dog is eyeing you up and down at every moment, determining your state of mind and how much leadership you have. If he doesn't perceive you as a leader, above him in rank, then anything you tell him is only a suggestion, which he can choose to ignore if it pleases him.

I can't tell you how many times I arrive at a new client's home and as they are rattling off the list of their dog's behavior problems they pause and glance down in surprise at their nice calm dog and say, "He's being real good now. But that's just because you're here. He knows you're a trainer."

Yes, he is behaving better because I'm there, but not because I'm a trainer. It's because a leader has just entered the room. I haven't even looked at the dog yet, all I did was enter the room confidently. That's the power and beauty of leadership - it can happen very quickly. Every time anyone enters a pack (this includes dogs, people and other animals) all dogs present are quickly determining where they fit in the new chain of command. As I enter the room, the dog quickly looks me over and determines that I am in a leadership position, my rank is above his, and he can't behave the way he does with his not-so-empowered owners.

Here's a quick example. I have a very typical Pit Bull, which means she loves everyone. The less she knows you the more she wants to say hi. I have one friend who's a little scared of dogs and he's the one my dog jumps on the most. Not because dogs can "smell fear," but because his body language reeks of uncertainty. My dog looks him over and quickly notices that his weight is on his back leg and his shoulders are rounded down slightly, which tells my dog that he has absolutely no leadership qualities, so she can do whatever she wants to do – and she wants to go say hello in a big way. Dogs don't "smell fear," they read your body like a book.

So the way to start being a leader is by standing up straight and moving with confidence, which is not an easy thing if you're not a very confident person. For some people it takes a lot of practice to get the hang of it. The problem is, you can only fake it for so long until your true feelings become apparent. And little Fido there will know it way before you do.

When I worked at Rover Ranch, a doggie daycare in New Jersey, I spent most of my time with the large dog packs. Day in and day out I would hang out with anywhere from four to fifteen dogs or so, most of whom were regulars. I can honestly say I had complete control over the pack every single day . . . except for one. One day I had no control – even though these were the same dogs that I was with every single day. That was day the day that my dog, Hayley, was getting surgery.

I entered the play area as I always did; I walked tall and with confidence and everything was looking good. After about ten minutes, I glanced at my watch and realized that Hayley was probably having her surgery at that exact moment. I'm sure my shoulders and head must have then slouched in worry. I was not aware that my body had changed at all, but every dog there recognized it immediately. They took one look at me and realized that I had become emotional; therefore I was no longer fit to be their leader. So they did what they had to do, what their instincts told them to do. They took over.

From the second I looked at my watch I lost control of the pack, and not a single dog would listen to me. For the next ten minutes I tried in vain to reclaim my position as leader and gain control of the dogs, which were now misbehaving and running wild. Finally, I came to realize what had happened, removed myself, and allowed a stable leader take my place. Like magic, order was soon restored. So don't think you can fool your dog – he always sees your true self. Every pack must have a leader to survive. If you're not fit for the position, your dog has no choice but to take the spot himself, even though he may not be qualified to fill it.

Your body language is only one ingredient in the recipe of leadership. Next, we add confidence. You must believe in yourself and your actions must reflect your belief. If your dog thinks that there is even the slightest hesitation on your part, he will know that there may be room for negotiation if he's persistent enough.

Not too long ago, I was meeting with a client who was having some problems with her little Maltese. As we went through the issues she was having with the dog she told me that he wouldn't go down the stairs no matter how hard she tried. She lived on the second floor and it was annoying to have to carry the dog down the stairs every single time they went out. He had no problems going up the stairs but he flatly refused to take the downward journey. My client told me she had tried everything and there was no way I was going to get him down those stairs. She even went so far as to bet me fifty dollars that I wouldn't be able to do it.

Sixty seconds later, I was in the money. All it took was simple leadership to show him that the stairs were no big deal. I first asked my client to show me how she attempted to get him down the stairs. She put his harness on and went down a few steps then looked back at him with what I would call a look of desperate pleading, and tentatively said, "Come on boy, come on." Her dog looked at the uncertainty in her eyes and the apprehension present in her body posture, and became instantly affected by it. He sensed that his human was nervous and unsure, and figured the reason for it must be the stairs before him. He's thinking, "These stairs always seem to make her a bit scared, they must be bad." The dog picked up on her energy and realized that she had absolutely no leadership qualities, and there was no way he was going to follow her down those stairs.

Now it was my turn. I picked up the leash, turned, and walked down the stairs without looking back. The dog balked as usual but instead of hesitating I moved forward with confidence. As the leash became taut I gave it a gentle tug (just enough to get his legs moving) and then released it. Without further resistance, the little guy followed me down to the bottom. I repeated this technique one more time, and then did it without the leash.

What my client had tried to do unsuccessfully for months using different kinds of tools, food and encouragement, I was able accomplish with leadership. Yes, I did use the leash as a tool (as did my client) to get him started, but it was only for that initial moment. That's how powerful and instantaneous leadership can be when executed properly. Our dogs are directly influenced by our actions and feelings at all times. It's the same with our children.

How many times have you seen a little boy trip and fall, and his mother runs over screaming, "Oh, my God, my little baby, are you okay!" The little boy then starts screaming his head off. However, if the same thing happens and mom just looks over and says calmly, "You're okay, get yourself back up," the boy brushes himself off and goes back to having fun. Both kids had the same experience, but now have different feelings about it due to their mom's energy, reaction, and leadership, or lack thereof.

For some reason, the term leadership has some bad connotations for various people, but it's merely a simple fact of canine life and without it your relationship with your dog will suffer. If you provide your dog with good, solid, and fair leadership, he will have the support he needs to feel comfortable and safe in your pack. Dogs crave that leadership and need the rules and boundaries provided by the top dog to be happy, well-balanced pooches. Keep in mind the battles over leadership are not physical, they are all psychological.

In the previous section, I discussed how important calm energy is for your dog and how your energy can directly affect your dog's behavior. As a leader, staying in a calm, composed frame of mind is imperative to properly communicating with your dog. Dogs will only follow stable leaders, period. If you become angry or frustrated, or feel sympathy or pity toward your dog, these emotions make you unstable as a leader and your dog has no choice but to take over. So no matter how crazy your dog is making you, or what kind of mistreatment they may have received before you got him, you must remain calm without letting your emotions get the best of you.

If you're ever watched Cesar Millan, aka "The Dog Whisperer", on television, you've heard him repeatedly talk about having calm, assertive energy with your dog. Cesar is a master at thinking like a dog, and he's really got it right when it comes to energy. If you're a very calm person, but also very laid back and passive, you aren't going to get through to your dog. And if you have no problem laying down the law and enforcing your rules but get excited and worked up easily, you're never going to communicate effectively. You must have the proper balance of being both calm and assertive to be a good leader.

A good human example of how all the aspects of leadership come together is Donald Trump. When Donald Trump walks into a room, he does so with supreme confidence. You know he's a powerful, successful man just by looking at him – his body language screams it. It doesn't matter if it's Bill Gates or Bill Clinton in the room; he thinks he is better than them. If a few people are having an argument, he calmly addresses them by stating, "You do this, you do this . . . and you're fired." He does this without getting worked up and without emotion. He says what he needs to say and moves on. When he tells someone to do something, there isn't a doubt in his mind that it won't be done. Every dog would follow Donald Trump.

This does not mean that you have to always be serious and stern whenever you are with your dog. There is plenty of time for fun and silliness throughout the day, but when rules are being enforced you need to assume the role of leader. Once you've established yourself as a stable, healthy leader, your rules and influence govern everything the dog does in your presence no matter where you go. I call this the "leadership umbrella". Wherever you and your furry best friend go, he always remains in your jurisdiction and is therefore subject to your rules. Once your leadership umbrella is up and looking good it makes it easy to teach your dog new rules that may arise as you visit new environments and encounter new situations.

A Word or Two about Dominance

The word dominance is being thrown around dog parks and vet offices like never before. I cringe every time I hear someone say that their dog is doing something because he's "trying to dominate them." Most people have no idea what dominance really means, and rarely are they a victim of "domination."

Dominance is really a very simple concept in the dog world. Every dog is either dominant or submissive to every other dog that enters the pack. If a dog is dominant over another dog, it means that he holds a higher rank and gets preference over resources. For example, if there is one bed in the room, the dominant dog has the right to it, if he so chooses, over any dog that is positioned beneath him in rank. It is neither a negative or positive concept, but merely a tool designed to keep order and structure within the pack.

When we humans enter the mix, we are included in the ranking system. If you do not show leadership qualities, your dog may see you as being subservient, therefore allowing him to seize the rank above you in the pack. If this is the case, then he will call the shots rather than you. Meaning, if he wants to sleep on the bed and you try to move him off, it is his right to tell you to back off (usually with a growl or snap). He's not trying to "dominate" you; he's simply reminding you who holds higher rank in the pack.

Instead of crucifying your dog for being "dominant over you" and trying to forcibly change his behavior, look at what you're doing (or not doing) and change your behavior. That's the only way you're going to show him that you're capable, qualified and deserving of the higher ranking spot in your pack.

4
Shut Up and Speak

Tell me if this sounds familiar: your dog does something that you don't approve of so you yell at him to stop, but he ignores you. So you yell louder and yank him away from whatever it is that he's not supposed to be doing. When you finally get him away and manage to get his attention you look down at him in frustration and think "What's wrong with you? Why don't you understand what I'm saying to you?" If you look closely, you'll notice those same questions in your dog's eyes.

The problem here is that we're speaking one language and our dogs are speaking another. I don't care how smart you think your dog may be, he will never be able to learn English. Yes, Fido can pick up quite a large number of words and connect them with various actions, but he will never truly comprehend all of the gibberish that's coming out of your mouth.

I'm sure there are some of you out there who right now are saying, "But my dog is sooo smart and I know he understands what I'm saying. I can just tell." Sorry, but no he cannot. I'm sure he's quite smart . . . the smartest dog ever . . . he's special . . . . Sorry, he still doesn't grasp most of what you're saying to him.

So that leaves it up to us to become fluent in the language of dog. To accomplish this, you need to be aware that dogs communicate in a very different way than we humans do. We are very dependent upon verbal speech as our main source of communicating, while dogs rarely use vocalizations to do their talking.

Since we are very verbal creatures, we tend to rely on spoken words whenever we need to communicate. This has taught our dogs one thing - we never shut up. We talk and talk and talk and talk all the time, and rarely does it have anything to do with them. We quickly become nothing more than background noise. So, if you want your dog to pay attention to you, talk to him like a dog and speak as little as possible. That way when you do make a quick vocalization to get his attention, it's not diluted in a string of chatter that he's already learned to tune out.

One word that never works is "no." How many times a day do you say "no"? Ten? Fifty? If you have kids, I guarantee it's well into the triple digits. I hate to break it to you, but "no" has lost all meaning to your dog. It's been said so many times that Fido has become numb to it. How the heck is your dog supposed to know that the first forty times you said "no" it wasn't meant for him, but now number forty-one is?

Now that speech is off the table, we have to really start thinking like dogs in order to get our message across. Dogs communicate with each other in three main ways: body language, eye contact, and physical presence. Once you learn when and how to use these three forms of communication, you and your dog will finally start to really understand each other.

There are going to be times when you're going to have to yell at your dog to get your message across, but to be effective, you must do it like a dog and yell with your eyes. That's right you read correctly, I told you to yell with your eyes. It may sound strange to us humans, but that's exactly how dogs argue with each other. Eye contact is a direct confrontation and a challenge. Two dogs staring at each other quietly, even from across the room, are having an argument. They will continue to argue until one of the dogs submits, which is done by simply looking away. Once one dog looks away the argument is over and both dogs move on. If the dogs are up for an argument and neither submits, then it gets physical.

Now, I don't want you to be on high alert and think every time Fido glances in your direction he's cursing you out. The overall context and situation in which the eye contact is given means everything. If Rover is looking at you but overall seems like a relaxed dog, chances are he just wants some affection. You need to look at the overall body language of your dog in addition to the eye contact to determine his true motives.

Open Your Eyes and Listen

Do you realize that your dog is having long, in depth conversations with you all the time? Well he is – you're just missing it. Dogs really are open books. They are constantly telling us how they feel and what they're thinking about. They hide nothing. It's all right there for you to see, if you know what to look for. Body language is the primary way in which dogs communicate with each other. They use their posture, facial expressions, ear and tail placements, as well as their overall energy, to tell the world what's on their mind. Dog's never do things "out of the blue," or "without warning." They let us know their state of mind at all times. You're just not deciphering his cues.

Dog body language is very complex and somewhat difficult to describe without visual observation, so for the purposes of this book I'm going to stick to the basics. However, I highly recommend you do some additional research by watching dogs in groups (or even two dogs interacting), or check out some of the great books out there on the subject which are loaded with lots of pictures. A general rule with dogs is the stiffer the dog, the more tension in the dog. Sounds pretty obvious, but you may have to watch carefully in order to make this distinction. Also, pay close attention to the mouth: an open mouth means a more relaxed dog, while a closed mouth can mean alertness or more tension.

The next time you're out for a walk with your dog watch him as he notices a squirrel nearby. Pay close attention to the changes in his body posture and facial features. If his mouth was open it will close, and his ears will go from being on the side or back to forward. You may also notice that he leans forward, sticking his chest out a bit. All of these signs tell you that your dog went from relaxed to alert and assertive. If it's a dog or a person at the other end of his gaze, you could be in for some trouble.

Now a stiff dog doesn't necessarily mean assertive, it could also mean anxiety or fear. If a stimulus that causes the dog to be wary presents itself, you will notice the same stillness, but instead of the dog's body moving up and forward it will typically move down and possibly back. Some dogs however, will remain motionless, frozen under circumstances which make them anxious or fearful. There is really no black or white here; there are many shades of gray. The whole stiff dog versus moving dog is only a general guideline, and the overall context of the situation, as well as the individual dog's behavior patterns, must also be taken into account.

Start to pay attention to your dog's body language at various times of the day. Watch his tail and ear placement when he is excited and playful, take note of his posture when meeting other dogs and people, and pay attention to eye contact and body assertiveness (leaning forward, remaining neutral and hesitating back). All of these observations will tell you exactly how your dog is feeling and enable you to begin to predict behavior based on his state of mind.

The most effective way to change unwanted behaviors is not to discipline the dog after he has already done something, but to correct him right before he does something. Timing is everything, and the only way to be able to act at the right time is to be able to read your dogs body, and identify the warning signs that will tell you the second his mind begins to go toward the behavior. It's the difference between stopping your dog from doing something and teaching him not to do something.

Personal Space, the Final Frontier

The third major way that dogs communicate is through personal space. Every dog has a bubble of space around them that is theirs, and needs to be respected. If a person or dog invades that space it can be seen as a challenge, or at the very least makes the dog a bit apprehensive (once again, depending on context). Dogs will encroach on another dog's bubble of space to take resources or just move them out of the way.

This bubble of space is especially important with shy and anxious dogs. These types of dogs really need their space to be respected and get very uncomfortable if it's invaded by anyone. Typically, dogs that have not been well-socialized will fit into this category. You need to take special care to respect their personal space at all times and allow them to move forward at their own pace, on their own terms. As soon as you invade another dog's bubble of space you automatically put them on the defensive.

The taking over of space is the best way claim a resource in the dog world. Let's say your dog jumps on the couch but you do not want Fido on the furniture. You need to communicate to him in a way that he can understand that you don't want him up there. So instead of yelling and screaming you need to calmly get him off the couch, then stand between him and the couch, blocking him from getting back on, and move him back a few feet by advancing into his bubble of space . He may try to maneuver around you, so be prepared for a little fancy footwork to deny him access past you.

Staying calm in this situation is critical. You must be moving as a leader and not as an additional source of energy. If your dog continues to move forward, you will move right at him, getting in his personal space and moving him back with your body. You are taking over the couch and the bubble of space around it. For young and persistent dogs, your "goaltending" could go on for a little while, but you must see it through. You know you've done your job when you can step aside, leaving a clear path to the couch but your dog does not take it. Congrats, you just claimed the couch. Now you control the resource and only you can determine if and when your dog will be allowed access.

If you have a dog that is shy around people, you need to make sure that his personal space is always respected. This will be especially difficult when you're walking your dog or if you are in any sort of public place. For some reason, most people don't think twice about charging over to pet a strange dog. Since your dog is attached to you by the leash and can't withdraw, it's up to you to make sure he has the space he needs to feel comfortable. You need to stop those approaching people immediately so that your dog never has to make the decision to defend itself (in this situation it's flight or fight and because of the leash, he only has one choice left). Shy dogs need to be the ones to make that first move forward when they feel comfortable. Having someone enter their space when they are not in a good frame of mind is only reinforcing their anxiety. They also need to trust you, as their leader, to always "have their backs" and to protect them when necessary.

Putting it All Together

Now that you know all about body language, eye contact, and physical presence, it's time to put these lessons into action. Let's say after of a long day of work and obligations you finally get a chance to plop down on the couch for some well deserved R & R. You take a deep breath, lean back and open up that great dog behavior book you've been reading. Just as you get to the bottom of the page, thinking what a genius this Fern guy is, your loving Labrador decides your expensive oriental rug looks pretty darn tasty and begins snacking on it.

Although you've never been all that fond of the rug (a gift from your mother-in-law), you still know that you need to address and correct your dog's behavior. Just before you scream out the word "no!" you remember something from that life-changing book in your hands and switch it to a "hey!" instead. And instead of yelling it, you loudly state it – kind of like a bark.

I know what you're thinking. I just finished telling you not to say anything and here I am telling you to say "hey." However, the way we're using it here is less like a word and more like a sound. It doesn't matter what sound you make either. The sound itself is really meaningless. Cesar Millan has made the "shhhhhht" sound popular and it works very well. Basically, you want to use a sound that you don't make in every day conversation. I use "hey," "shhhhht," and "ehh" interchangeably. When my dog hears any one of these three sounds, she knows I'm talking to her. There is never any confusion because I only use those sounds for her and her alone.

The sound is used to do two things. First, it lets the dog know the instant he's making a mistake – even if you're across the room from him. Second, it's a tool to obtain eye contact. Without eye contact, don't even bother trying to communicate with your dog. Dog's pretty much have one track minds, and are only thinking about whatever they're looking at. If your dog isn't looking at you, you can bet he's forgotten you're even there. Getting that eye contact is like hearing a dial tone. Without it, you can yap all you want but there's no one on the other end to hear you.

So you say "hey!" to mark your dog's bad behavior and attempt to gain eye contact. If you were successful and your dog turned toward you, that might be it. A stable leader only uses the minimum amount of correction necessary. On this day, however, your dog is really into the carpet and totally ignores you, so you have to go further. You assume a more dominant position by confidently standing nice and tall, and then calmly and assertively walk over to your dog.

As you reach him and enter his space, and he finally looks up at you as if he just realized that you were in the room with him. You walk into his space, staring down at him, forcing him to back-pedal a few feet and then stop. Your dog stops with you and looks up. Noticing his body language, you quickly assess that he doesn't seem like he will lunge forward if you weren't there, so you move calmly back to the couch. Your message seems to have been delivered successfully because he's still calmly standing where you left him, respecting the invisible wall you just put up before him.

You may have to repeat this process if your dog heads back over to resume his munching. If this is the case, you must continue this cycle for as long as it takes for him to give up. It's easy to get frustrated when instead of relaxing, you're continually getting up from the couch, however, if you stay the course and get your dog to finally submit, the next time you have a similar disagreement with him it won't take quite as long. You must follow through until you get what you want though. If you give up too early, the next encounter will take twice as long.

By working on using your eyes instead of your mouth, being aware of your dog's body language, and learning to use personal space when conversing with your poochy pal, I think you'll soon discover that the lines of communication will begin to open up and your relationship with your dog will improve greatly. There may be a bit of a learning curve before you feel completely comfortable using this new form of communication, but if you can apply it correctly, you and your dog may finally begin to understand each other.

5
But it's Raining Outside

You're not going to believe it, but I'm about to spend a whole chapter talking about exercise. Everyone out there knows that dogs need exercise, right? Of course you do. So, why then, do so few people exercise their dogs adequately?

One of the things I ask in every single behavior session is, "How much exercise does the dog get?" Although it's one of the most important questions in troubleshooting problem behaviors, I really don't care what the answer is. Whatever I'm told, it's not enough.

Believe it or not, most behavior problems will significantly diminish if the dog is properly exercised. It really can be that simple because a tired dog is a good dog. If your dog is pooped out, then he's too tired to chew up your furniture, bark at the window all day, or raid the kitchen garbage. If he's good and exercised, he's laying down relaxing like a good boy. I'll say it again: a tired dog is a good dog – always!

The big problem for us is that the human world comes with obligations and responsibilities that prohibit us from spending all day tiring out our dogs. But Rover can't forget about his needs just because it's raining outside or because we have to go to work.

All dogs wake up with energy. As soon as they get up in the morning - BANG - it's there, and they are very aware of it. No matter what they do they can't get it out of their minds.

It's like if you woke up in the morning and had to put on a pair of glasses covered with spots. No matter what you do during the day, you have to wear the glasses at all times. Sure, you can do the things you normally do, like make breakfast and go to work, but the spots are always there, right in your face. It probably wouldn't take long for those spots to make you more than a little nuts. Then imagine the relief you would feel when the spots finally clear.

Dogs must release that energy in some way – they have no choice. So the question then becomes, how will Rover release that energy while we're at work for eight hours a day? He may see how good the drapes taste or dig a nice hole in the carpet or maybe even do a little redecorating around the house. Whatever Rover's choice, we're probably not going to be smiling when we open the front door at the end of the day.

Typically, the younger the dog, the bigger the energy tank. Therefore, it becomes more important that his energy be released constructively. Your dog cannot just forget about that energy, it has to be let out somehow. That's why you'll see many puppies just run around the living room in circles at warp speed for a few minutes and then just collapse, panting. The energy just takes over and your little pup is powerless against its control.

Some dogs will need much more exercise than others. Breed and individual personality play a huge factor here. If you go out and get a Jack Russell Terrier puppy because you thought Eddie on *Fraiser* looked cute and you happen to live in a small Manhattan apartment, boy are you in for a surprise. A dog like that requires about three hours of sprinting a day – minimum. If you have a sedate ten year old English Bulldog, however, a lap around the couch may wipe him out for half the day.

In general, we humans grossly underestimate the exercise requirements of our dogs. When someone tells me that they give their dog plenty of exercise by taking it for three "long" (10-15 minute) walks a day, I find it very hard to hide my laugh. This barely takes the edge off what your dog is really craving.

You must recognize the true exercise needs of your dog, and then do something about it. I don't want to hear you complain about your dog's behavior problems if you're very aware that he doesn't get enough exercise yet do nothing about it. Remember, it's a basic canine need and it must be addressed on a daily basis.

Whatever problems you may be having with your dog, exercise can play a huge role in diminishing them. If your dog is tired, he doesn't have the energy to get into trouble, and any conflicts which arise will be remedied much quicker. Many of the behavior sessions I get called in on could be concluded by my simply walking into the house, saying, "Exercise your dog more," and then walking out. It really can have that big an impact.

OK, So Now What?

We agree that you're not getting your dog enough exercise and to help him be a happy, healthy pooch in your world you need to get him more. However, we all have jobs, responsibilities, school, happy hour, must-see-TV . . . and so on and so on. Unlike our dogs, our world is very complicated, packed tight with many obligations – some important, others not so much.

The time has come to do some prioritizing in your life and decide just how important your dog is to you. Since you cared enough to buy this book, I'm guessing your dog ranks fairly high. So you care about your dog and have come to the realization that he deserves better, and you want to give him the energy outlet he really needs. But how?

There are a number of great ways to exercise your dog that will fit into your lifestyle and interests. You just need to try some different things and see what works best for you and your dog.

The first thing I recommend is to get your butt out of bed thirty minutes earlier each day. Will missing that half hour of sleep each day kill you? No, it won't – and those thirty minutes could make all the difference to your dog. If we use that time to give our dogs a quick energy outlet first thing in the morning, we're helping our dogs start the day off on the right track and clear some of those spots from in front of their eyes.

Taking your dog for a walk is good for so many reasons (see next chapter) and although it's not exactly high-impact exercise, it's always a solid choice. For older dogs, walking is the best and sometimes only real exercise option. Let the physical condition of your dog dictate the pace and terrain of your walk. If you're walking for exercise purposes, don't feel bad about not letting him sniff every single tree you pass. When you're taking a casual stroll, you can let him sniff to his doggie heart's content. Just remember that you set the pace and are in control of the walk, and make sure your dog sticks to your agenda.

A great way to make your dog work a little harder while on your typical walk is by adding a backpack – to him, not to you. If you've never seen one, it looks pretty much like a human backpack complete with compartments and bungees for holding lots of stuff. By adding a little weight to your dog, you can double the effectiveness of his energy output. Put him to work and make him carry your keys, water bottle and clean up bags.

Make sure you start him off light, probably with just the pack alone to let him get used to the feeling. Then, add a little weight each day, but make sure you don't overdo it – he's a dog not an SUV. Also, try to make sure you distribute the weight evenly on each side of the pack.

Adding a backpack is especially useful if you have any of the working breeds. Man has bred working dogs to do specific jobs and they don't really feel fulfilled unless they have a job to do. You'll notice the difference as soon as you put the pack on your dog. You'll see him concentrate on the weight on his back, and he is usually less distractible.

Doing breed-specific exercise is a great way to let your dog get rid of that energy and fulfill his breeding instincts at the same time. Bernese Mountain Dogs, for example, were bred to pull carts, so adding a backpack or even letting them pull a wagon will give them the satisfaction of doing what they are genetically encoded to do. For any scent hound, like a Beagle, I like to play "Find It." You get a Kong (which is a great hollow rubber toy you can find in any pet store) and stuff it with something tasty. Make sure it's something that the dog will have to spend some time getting out (peanut butter works well – even better if you freeze it in the Kong). Then you put your dog into a sit/stay position, and place the object partially behind a piece of furniture, so the dog can just barely see it. Then say "find it," and release your dog so that he can get it and spend the next fifteen minutes enjoying his snack. Every day that you do this, you hide the Kong a little better, making your dog really use his nose to sniff it out. This is great fun for rainy days with any dog and you can use any treat as the treasure. Just make sure that it takes some time for your dog to eat it.

Obviously, jogging or bike riding with your furry companion will up the exertion level and relieve more energy than a walk during the same amount of time. If you have any kind of terrier, I highly recommend you opt for the speedier exercise methods. Make sure you work on your leash skills before you start a jogging or biking regimen with your dog. If you can't control him while you're on a walk, there's no way you're going to survive upping the pace with a jog or bike ride.

"Fetch" is a favorite of many dogs and is a great way to get you pooch really moving. You don't really need a big area to play it in either. Of course, if you have access to a large outdoor area where you can get your dog sprinting, that would be ideal, however, an indoor hallway can work, as well. If your dog is a fetchaholic, like mine, he'll be more than happy to play the game anywhere and everywhere.

Swimming is probably one of the best forms of exercise for your dog. For a dog that likes playing fetch, the water version is a blast. There is little that can rival the exertion your dog will get by canon-balling into the water and swimming back to you (again and again and again). It's great for older dogs, too (the swimming, not the fetch). The water supports most of their weight and gives the senior dog a nice rest from gravity while still allowing them to move those bones.

Always remember safety first, especially in the water. Don't expect that your dog knows how to swim and just dump him into the pool. Ease him in and see how he does, and never leave your dog in the water unattended. If you have an in-ground pool take the time to bring your dog in the pool and teach him how to get out. Swim with him, showing him where the stairs are, and make sure he can use them on his own. Accidents happen, and if he unexpectedly ends up in the pool one day, you'll want to be confident that he can get himself out.

Even if your dog can't swim (there are some breeds that are just not made for it) he can still enjoy the fun of the water. They make great doggie life jackets that will keep Fido afloat, allowing him to swim, or at least bob like a buoy, and cool off. There is also a wide assortment of fun and interactive dog toys that are made especially for aquatic canine enjoyment.

If you don't have a lot of space or are trapped indoors, bubbles can be loads of fun for your dog. Just get the non-toxic kind you can find in most toy stores, and let Fido jump and lunge after them in your living room. You'd be surprised how worked up some dogs will get as they jump around snapping at all of those strange looking orbs.

Even though all of the above methods of exercising your dog are good, none of them compare to letting your dog play with another dog. When your pooch gets together with his doggie buddies, he'll get to play like he was meant to: like a dog. They will take turns chasing each other around and around, then pouncing and mouthing each other with wild exuberance. Then they'll roll around on the ground in a big, tumbling mound of excited yelps. Now that's exercise! I've watched dogs play for hours and I always find myself feeling exhausted just from watching all the fun. There's nothing better than letting your dog take a break from the human world and allowing him to get in touch with his canine roots. It's natural, it's healthy, and it's a definite canine need.

Dog parks are great ideas in theory; however, they are filled with uncertainty. You are taking a big leap of faith by assuming that every dog is healthy, and that every owner is responsible. Given the right mix of dogs and humans the dog park is a canine utopia. Unfortunately, it really only takes one bad dog or one stupid human to ruin it for everyone.

We all bring our emotional baggage to the dog park with us and impart it onto our dogs. If you're anxious or nervous for any reason while in the dog park, you are sending out a lot of unstable energy that every dog is aware of. This can adversely affect the behavior of the pack. As always, it's important to set good examples for our dogs in any situation. If you're projecting nice, calm energy, they will be influenced by your confidence and be better dogs inside and out.

So use dog parks responsibly, and if your dog seems to regularly get into trouble there, maybe the dog park isn't right for him. Go out and get yourself a good trainer, and see if it's something that you can work him through. But don't be that one person who is souring the experience for everyone.

Since dog parks are kind of a gamble, I like the option of doggie daycare instead. In a doggie daycare, you eliminate many of the unknowns that exist in dog parks. You know for a fact that every dog at the daycare is relatively healthy and up-to-date on vaccines. Every dog has been temperament tested to make sure he gets along with other dogs and will enjoy the environment. Most importantly, you remove the human element and all the baggage that can come with it. The pack is supervised by a neutral, unbiased person who makes sure every dog is behaving, obeying the rules, and having fun.

Another option that is often overlooked is giving Rover some mental exercise. Teaching your dog obedience commands or tricks can really work his noggin and strengthen your bond with him, as well as tire him out mentally. Think back to when you had to study for a big test in school. All that concentration could really wipe you out after a while. By working on some commands or tricks, you learn better communication with your dog, stimulate his brain, and give your dog a constructive outlet for all that energy. Your dog gets to spend some quality time with you and gets lots of yummy treats –it's a win-win for both you and your dog.

Taking any kind of group class is a great exercise option in the winter when most of us are slacking on getting our dogs out and running. If you've got a very energetic dog an agility class is the answer to your dog's prayers. Learning to run an agility course with your dog is very fulfilling for both dog and handler, is a top notch energy releaser and is just plain fun.

With so many choices out there to get your dog the exercise he needs, there is just no excuse for not giving him an outlet for his energy. I know we're all busy, but we brought dogs into our homes with the understanding that we would have to take care of them – not according to our human agenda, but according to their individual canine needs. So I want everyone reading this right now to do whatever you have to do get your dog more exercise on a daily basis, no matter how much he's currently getting. Whatever you're doing for him now, step it up. By draining his energy, you're doing yourself and your dog a huge favor, and helping to ensure that you will be together forever.

6
These Paws
Were Made For Walking

Wild canines as well as homeless domestic dog packs will spend a good portion of their time walking. They'll patrol their territory as well as go on exploratory walks pretty much all day long. Why, you ask? Well, because walking is a definite canine need and, like it or not, that's what dogs do. Walking is where a dog pack really comes together, strengthening their bonds with one another and fortifying the group structure.

For dogs, there is something very therapeutic about the ritual of walking. In addition to exercise and leadership, walking your dog is always part of the solution for almost all problem behaviors. Done properly, the walk is a great leadership exercise and a way to help you bond with your furry pal. When you and your dog are walking side by side in a nice rhythm together, you become united as a team, enjoying both the environment and each other.

Many of us see the act of walking our dog as nothing more than quick bathroom break for him and an annoying chore for us. Once you understand what the walk really means to your dog and open your mind to the experience, you can change your perspective and enjoy sharing this time together with your dog. Let's not forget that walking is good for us humans, as well.

Instead of seeing the walk as an obligation, look at it as an opportunity to take a moment out of your crazy day and enjoy some time with your dog. Devote yourself to your four-legged best bud with nothing else on your mind. Don't worry about all the work waiting for you at the office; or the family and household commitments that are still undone; or the fight you had with your spouse that morning. All of that stuff will be there when you get back. For now, take a deep breath and look down at your dog. He couldn't be happier to be going out for a walk with you, and there isn't anything else in world that he would rather be doing. Like everything else, go into the walk with an open mind and be willing to allow yourself to really enjoy it.

Initially, it's going to take a lot of conscious effort on your part to leave all your worries at home, but if you keep reminding yourself what the walk is supposed to be about, I think you'll see that your mind will eventually forget about all those human distractions. Once that happens, you'll find yourself smiling as much as your dog.

To really take advantage of what the walk can accomplish, it needs to last a bit longer than what the typical dog owner sees as a walk. Chances are you and your dog have very different ideas about how long a walk should be. I'm always surprised at how many people think that a spin around the block is a good walk. Most dogs would have no problem walking for hours and traveling for miles but, unfortunately, we eventually have to get back to the "real world" before too long. So you need to compromise and do the best you can with your individual schedule. Ideally, you should try to get the average dog out for at least one thirty minute walk a day and a couple of one hour walks a week. More would be better, but I understand that it may not be a realistic goal for the average person, so I'm making that my minimum.

Walk Like a Dog

Now that you've decided to embrace walking your dog and are committed to spending at least a half hour cruising the neighborhood, seeing the local sites and perhaps partaking in a little butt sniffing, allow me (or more specifically, your dog) to teach you how to walk. While we take the walk for granted, our dogs revel in every smell, sight and sound. To them, it's not just passing the time, it's a sensory carnival.

The first thing to remember is that your dog is going on your walk, not the other way around. Sometimes you'll want to walk at a brisk pace, while other times you may want to slowly stroll, letting your dog sniff away at his leisure. Just make sure you've perfected your leash walking and he's not dragging you all over the place. I'm not going to get into how to train your dog to walk on a leash here. I feel for something like that, you need to have a hands-on lesson where you can learn exactly how to work with your individual dog. But for now, know that your leash should be relaxed and not taut like a trapeze wire.

The walk is a big reward for your dog, and like all things he values, it's only given when he's in a calm state of mind. So make sure you take the time to switch him from excited to calm before you even open the door. Once he's calm, out you go.

When you get outside, stop and take a minute to take a deep breath. As you inhale, smell the air and try to identify each individual smell as it hits your nose. Then listen to the different sounds around you: birds, street noise, and the rattle of the tags on your dog's collar. Lastly, look around and take note of your surroundings. Look at the multitude of colors around you and pay attention to small details that you would normally overlook.

That's a small window into how your dog experiences the outdoor world. Ted Kerasote does a great job of explaining how dogs "see" things in his book *Merle's Door*. When writing about the first time he met Merle, this big, yellow stray Labrador, he describes his impression of the dog visually (as is the human way), while he describes the dog's first impression of him by smell alone.

The dog world is ruled by the nose, and that's their main tool when they're out on a walk. So although we are a visually dependant species, I want you to try really hard to use your nose while walking with your dog. Why, you ask? Because if look down at your dog at any time during your walk I think you'll notice how happy he looks. Most of the time we're so preoccupied with ourselves that we rush the entire process of the walk, sometimes barely aware of what's happening.

Think about the last walk you took with your dog. Can you remember the color of any of the houses you passed? Do you know what kind of cars drove by? What did you smell? Cut grass? Pizza from a nearby restaurant? These are questions I know your dog could answer. My point here is that both you and your dog were on the same walk, however, only one of you really soaked it in and opened up to the simple fun of it. Even if you love taking walks with your dog and have a smile on your face the entire time, you can still take it up a notch and walk more like a dog.

A good way to keep it interesting for both of you is to never go the same way twice in a row. Make each walk as different as possible, allowing exposure to a variety of smells, sights and sounds. Every time you allow your dog to stop and do some sniffing, you do the same. Take a deep breath and open your senses. Notice the things around you, and enjoy an actual experience, not just a time-filler. If you make the extra effort to practice walking more like a dog, I think you'll find that you'll enjoy the break from the human world and become closer to your traveling companion.

If you like the experience, and want to take the canine walk experience to the next level, gather some of you and your dog's pals and walk together in a pack. Now that's walking like a dog! There's nothing more canine than dogs walking together in a pack. That's where dogs really come together and live life as they were designed to by nature.

Walking dogs together is also one of the best ways to introduce dogs to each other. Since we know all about eye contact from the earlier chapter on communication, we know that we want to avoid head-on eye contact as much as possible. By getting the dogs moving in the same direction, you help them to feel more comfortable and instantly unify them. Now, instead of two or more separate packs, they become one single unit.

I believe walking dogs together in a pack is incredibly beneficial to the mental well-being of all domestic dogs. Dogs are not solitary in nature; they are pack animals that are innately drawn to form groups of their own kind. I've used pack walks as a tool to help many dogs suffering from a variety of behavior problems including fear, anxiety and aggression. Pack walks let dogs tap into their canine roots, helping them to overcome some of the issues bestowed upon them by the human world. Basically, it's dogs helping dogs to be dogs.

The bottom line is that walking is good for your dog no matter what breed or personality you have sitting there on the couch next to you. They all crave the great outdoors (although some breeds do have climate restrictions) and desire to stroll with their packs, exploring their world one sniff at a time. As their caregivers and guardians, it's up to us to make time to give them the walks they need and deserve. Our dogs, in return, will show us how to take a moment away from the stress of our human lives and experience the walk as they do – with wagging tails and smiling faces.

7
Your Dog's "Thing"

No matter when you get your dog, or how much training you do with him, odds are there will always be certain aspects of your dog's personality that will require your ongoing attention. Some dogs are shy around certain people; others are chronic barkers; while others may chase squirrels, no matter what you do to deter them. How much attention these annoying trouble areas will need depends on a number of factors.

Many dogs develop issues because of an event (either single or repetitive) that happened to them as a puppy. The event may not seem like a big deal to us, but if your puppy perceives it as traumatic, the effect can stay with him forever unless something is done to change that perception. It could be something as trivial as an object falling off of a table, startling the pup. If he then receives inappropriate affection (see chapter 9), it can cause him to fear that object or sound. Perhaps, the puppy was constantly yelled at by a man during the first few months of his life. That can easily lead him to become wary, fearful or aggressive toward all men.

Your dog's individual personality will probably play the biggest role in all of his behaviors. If you've got a high energy, short attention span, ever-playful pooch, he will be inclined toward the obvious slew of behavior problems. Meanwhile, if you've got a lounging couch potato, his mellow laziness can lead to other issues.

Breed can also be a huge factor in some common behavioral issues. Humans have bred certain dogs to do specific jobs, and through selective breeding have been very successful in designing great working dogs. These dogs are born with the innate desire to fulfill their breeding and do their assigned jobs. If you bring home a Border Collie, don't be surprised if he runs after your kids while they're playing in the back yard, and nips at their ankles. He's not misbehaving; he's only doing his job as a herding dog.

His level of desire to do that job depends a lot on each dog's individual genetics. If your dog's parents were great herding dogs, chances are that your pup will be born to herd, too. If you've got a terrier, don't be surprised when he chases small animals; if you best bud is a Beagle, be prepared to watch him wander off every time he catches a good scent; and if your share your life with a Doberman Pinscher, he will most likely let you know the second anyone steps foot on your property.

There is no way to overwrite your dog's breeding. It's coded into his DNA, and will always be there no matter how much training you do. It's like telling an eighteen-year-old boy not to look at girls, and then sending him to a bikini contest. He knows you instructed him not to look, but every fiber of his being is screaming at him to point his peepers at those girls. He's going to look – no doubt about it – and your dog, likewise, will always do what his breeding is yelling at him to do. What we need to be concerned with is how quickly we can get them focused back on us.

Whatever your dog's breed, personality, or upbringing, he will most likely have that one ongoing concern that takes up the bulk of your training time. Every dog has its "thing". This is the one thing (although some of you lucky people may have a dog with multiple things) that you are always working on with your dog, and can sometimes work on for his entire life.

Try not to get mad or resentful towards your dog because he has this ongoing issue. Hey, we all have our issues, but that doesn't mean we're bad people, and the same goes for our dogs. That's just the area in which our dog needs our help the most, and it's up to us to give him the assistance he needs to fit in to our world. Don't think it's just your dog either. Every dog out there has its thing; some are just more obvious than others. So accept this, and work with your dog to help him manage his thing and be a well-adjusted member of your pack.

Aggression

There are many forms of aggression, and I strongly believe that you should seek out the help of a qualified professional to evaluate the situation and assist you in your dog's rehabilitation. For now, I'll go over the three big ones (aggression toward people, dogs, and food aggression) and give some initial advice on treatment, but I recommend you contact a local dog behavior specialist as soon as possible.

The term aggression seems to have a different meaning to everyone. For me, true aggression is when a dog bites and holds on, has to be physically removed from its target, and has caused physical injury. However, for most dog owners, aggression is used to describe any assertive behavior of your dog that includes growling, snarling, snapping, and biting toward a human or dog.

Aggression toward people can be exclusive to specific types (men, children, or certain ethnic groups), or be directed at everyone. Most cases of dog aggression that I see are due to a fear, insecurity, or anxiety. To appropriately treat aggression, we need to first try to determine what is triggering it. This may not always be easy, and may take some investigative skills. If you're not sure what is causing it, you need to pretend you're a CSI detective and start searching for clues. Replay the recent incidents when your dog showed signs of aggression, and look for the common factors throughout them all.

One element to watch out for is yourself. If your dog seems to only show aggression toward people (and/or dogs) when you are present, it tells me there is probably a leadership issue in your pack. Your dog has taken the role as leader, and actually sees you as his possession. As leader, he feels it's his job to protect what is his from anyone that approaches.

Typically, the dog will only react if he is between the owner and an approaching person (or dog). However, I've also seen cases where spouses couldn't even hug, no matter where the dog was in the room. These types of dogs will often guard other resources such as food, toys, and sleeping areas.

What needs to happen in this case is that the owner needs to step up and show the dog that he has a leader and that protection is not his job. If this sounds like you, do lots of leadership exercises and make sure everything your dog values comes through you, and is on your terms. You may also need to assess how you are communicating to your dog, and make sure he's getting the message properly when you're giving corrections.

If your dog is wary of all people, in all circumstances, we need to change his perception of people from unwanted intruder to welcome guest baring yummy gifts. I started to write some specific instructions on how to deal with such situations, but then decided it's probably best not to. Every dog's issues are very specific and treatment will greatly depend on the severity of the problem, attitude of the owner, and ability to control the situation. I feel if I give specific instructions to deal with some of these cases, they may be taken out of context, and possibly result in injury.

There is just too much to consider before you can implement a treatment plan, and properly execute it. You always need to recognize your dog's level of sensitivity, and work within that threshold. The progress will be at your dog's pace, not yours, so be patient. The key is taking the time to allow your dog to get to a calm state of mind – no matter how long that takes. We need to break his usual cycle of behavior, and show your dog that there is a different way to behave around the people he normally reacts to.

Controlling the environment is crucial to success. You need to always try to set up the situation so you can succeed in changing your dog's state of mind. This is often very difficult to do, especially when you're out on a walk, and have no control over the other people you encounter. Don't attempt to work on something unless you know it will end favorably. If you don't have the time, or can't control the situation, don't even try.

Food aggression is another serious problem that, without question, must be addressed – especially if there are young children in your family. Dogs that guard their food will often react aggressively around all resources, but it can be localized to food alone. The reason he is guarding his food is that he feels he needs to guard it in order to keep it, and it usually works for him.

Food aggression comes in a wide range of severity, and the treatment of each depends on each individual case. Basically, your dog has something he values, and if he growls or snaps and keeps possession of it, he's rewarded for it. I DO NOT want you to go and try to take it away from him, and risk getting bitten. As with all forms of aggression, this is where a professional with experience in dealing with this kind of thing is so important. Your safety is always the first priority.

So, I'm not going to go into how you would take something away from him, although, depending on the dog, that is sometimes part of my treatment plan. Instead, I want you to work on making your dog love it when you are around his food.

The first step is to start hand-feeding your dog his meals. Get his bowl full of food and put it on the counter, and let him eat only a small portion out of your hand at a time. After a few days (or weeks) of that, fill his bowl and hold it for him as he eats, keeping the bowl off the floor. Every ten seconds or so, lift the bowl up, have him wait patiently for a moment, and lower it back down for him to eat again. Continue this until his meal is done.

Once you're successful with this technique, fill his bowl, put it on the floor, stand up, and stay there with a bag of high-impact treats, like grilled chicken or steak. Every few seconds, drop a piece into his bowl. Repeat this for a few more days. Then do the same thing, but lower your hand toward the bowl a bit before you drop the treat. Slowly, move down until you are placing the food in your dog's bowl. There is no specific timeline for these steps, and all of this is only done if, and only if, your dog is cool with it. If he is showing any signs of aggression back up a step and/or consult a professional.

I was very reluctant to include aggression treatment in this book because if anything is done incorrectly, you can get bitten and possibly seriously injured. There's a lot involved in treating a serious problem like aggression. I can't emphasize enough how important it is to address aggression issues as soon as possible with a qualified dog behavior specialist. Nothing will improve unless you are very proactive, and do the right things to help your dog work through these issues.

Anxiety or Fear

You are much more likely to get bit by a fearful or anxious dog than by an aggressive dog. This is because the aggressive dog will be giving off very obvious signals of his intentions, while a fearful or anxious dog may not. Learning a bit about canine body language will help you recognize when your dog is telling you that he's not comfortable with a situation. Typical signs of anxiety and fear are ears back or tucked down, tail curled between legs, frozen body and facial features, lowering of head and body, tongue flicks (licking the air), panting, and avoidance behaviors. These signs could be very obvious or only mildly noticeable depending on the level of your dog's reaction. You always need to recognize and respect how your dog is feeling at all times.

I think there is nothing sadder than a dog (or person, for that matter) living with unnecessary phobias, because it can so drastically affect their quality of life. To me, a dog who is fearful or anxious is crying out for help, and it's our duty to do everything we can to help him through his issues, allowing him to enjoy everything this life has to offer.

If you do have a dog with anxiety issues, you should know that it's never a quick fix. Treatment can be slow and ongoing, but great results are definitely possible. Like all behavior issues, the longer a problem has been going on, the longer it takes to address, so don't delay. As with aggression, I really believe enlisting the assistance of a qualified professional is worth every penny here. If you don't do things just the right way, or push your dog too fast or too far, you can make the problem much worse.

If your dog is shy, or shows signs of anxiety around people (all or specific types) you need to go over what you learned about leadership and your body language, and pretty much do the opposite. You don't want to stand tall, make direct eye contact, and get into your dog's space. Instead, you want to never directly face him, never make direct eye contact with him, and give him as much space as he needs.

You'll want to find the distance where the dog is aware of the person, but not shutting down with fear. Then, just casually hang out, while your volunteer occasionally tosses your dog a very tasty snack (the higher the level of the dog's reaction, the better the treat), always making sure that the person never looks over at him. If the dog is taking the food, then he's not that scared. If he won't take any food, the person is too close.

Make sure your dog is not cornered during this exercise and has enough space behind him to back away a bit, if he feels too uncomfortable. For bad cases, that may be all you do for a while (days, even weeks). The goal is to start throwing the treats closer and closer, as long as the dog continues to advance, until the person is able to hand feed him. Never, under any circumstances, have them reach out and touch the dog. The dog must always be the one to make the first move. Be patient and understand how difficult this may be for your dog. If the person tries to touch him too soon, you will have ruined all the good work you did, and most likely have to go back to the beginning to gain back the dog's trust.

As you already know, I'm a big fan of walking dogs. Walking anxious dogs with other dogs and people is a great way to help them experience a different frame of mind, in the presence of what usually makes them nervous. Remember that eye contact, and directly facing an anxious dog is very confrontational, so by walking together in the same direction, you will help your dog feel more at ease. The walk will also unify everyone as pack mates and help your fearful Fido to think of people in a different way. If your dog is anxious of other dogs, nothing helps like a pack walk, provided the dogs you're walking with are relatively well mannered and respectful of his space.

This will also help with dog-dog aggression. Before you can get everyone walking together though, you will have to work with the aggressive dog, changing his state of mind, before bringing him next to the other dogs. Start as far away as you need to, and slowly work your way toward the other dogs, until you are directly behind them. Then, as long as you feel confident that you can control the dog, move him in line with the pack. You may have to work through some lunging, and defuse some aggressive behavior, but if you get the dog through it, you can show him a new state of mind and behavior around other dogs. Although you may never take him to dog parks, you can certainly have him around other dogs without going ballistic.

Dogs can also develop a fear of an object or situation. Anything from fireworks, to garbage cans, to specific noises. To help your dog get over this kind of fear, most of the things we just talked about will still apply. Find the distance and/or intensity of the thing that makes your dog anxious, where he is aware of it, but not completely shutting down. The rule for food-motivated dogs is that if he will take a treat, he's not that scared, and that's the point at which you want to work with him.

Walk him back and forth near the object, or if it's a sound, with the sound at low volume, and dole out some treats. You can go through some commands or tricks that your dog knows, to occupy his mind with something other than concentrating on the thing that has him spooked. Work with him until you are able to see a change in his state of mind. He doesn't have to be completely relaxed; he just needs to show some improvement.

As always, don't rush things. Take your time, and recognize when your dog has had enough. You always want to end on a good note, and when he is in a calm state of mind.

Separation Anxiety

Dogs are social, group animals that, given the choice, will always want to be with their pack mates. That's natural and to be expected. However, because the human world will present times when your dog must be left by himself, he also needs to be confident and accepting of spending time alone. Even if you spend every day with your dog, or have other dogs living at home, your dog needs to be comfortable being independent as well.

The first thing you have to do in regard to separation anxiety is to let go of your emotional attachment to your dog for a moment, and realize what's really best for him. Separation anxiety is created by us, and nurtured by our misunderstanding of our dog's needs.

Your dog has to adapt to your lifestyle and routines, which will include being left alone from time to time. You should not feel bad about it, or carry around guilt because if it. It's just the way life is, and both you and your dog need to accept that. If you are emotional because you have to leave your dog to go to work, to dinner, even the mailbox, your dog will feel it and reflect that emotional instability.

Your dog's state of mind has never been more important than with this issue. Be very conscious of your dog's state of mind whenever you give affection, and only give him all that love and attention when he's in a calm mindset. This is especially important when you leave or come back home. Stop all big hellos and goodbyes.

Your coming and going has to be a non-event. If you make a big fuss when you come into your house and gush over your dog, you're sending him the message to take notice of this event – something big just happened. If, before you leave the house, you throw yourself at your dog saying, "I'm going to miss you sooo much, my fuzzy little buddy. Momma's going to miss you sooo much," you're telling your dog that you're an emotional mess at what is happening, and they should make note of it.

Coming and going has to be no big deal. When you have to leave, you pick up your keys, give a quick wave to your dog and walk out. That's it. No baby talk, no hugs, no emotion, just walk out. To make things a little easier on you and your dog, make sure he's been adequately exercised before you go out (if possible), and leave him something to do while you leave. Give him a stuffed Kong, or something inter-esting to chew on, so that he's occupied while you head out. What-ever you give him, make sure it will take him at least fifteen minutes to go through. Stuffing Kongs with moistened kibble or peanut but-ter, and then freezing it is a great choice that will keep your pooch happily munching during the time he normally goes nuts. You can also feed your dog his meals this way, by using a few Kongs.

Then when you come home, I want you to do the unthinkable: ignore your dog. Oh, how could I be so cruel? I must have a heart of stone. Sorry, hate me if you want, but ignore your dog when you first come back home. I want you to always enter your house like you're carrying two big bags of groceries. Don't look at your dog, don't speak to your dog – pretend you have no dog. Go to the kitchen counter and look through your mail, or read a magazine, and wait. Wait for as long as it takes for your dog to go from an excited, anxious, crazy state of mind, to a calm one. Once he's calm, then you can go ahead and give him a nice hello.

If you do that, you're rewarding a calm state of mind and down-play-ing the event of your coming home. It may only take five minutes, or it can last quite a bit longer. No matter how long it takes, you wait for that calm state of mind. With repetition and consistency, you'll see that the time it takes for him to get to a calm state of mind is steadily decreasing. The exception to this rule is if you think your dog has to go to the bathroom. In that case, take him right out, but be very non-chalant about it. For those of you who crate your dog while you're out, ignore him as described above, and only let him out of the crate when he's calm.

If you have a "Velcro" dog, that seems to never leave your side, and follows you everywhere from the bathroom to your bed at night, you must begin to pay less attention to your dog. I know, I'm an insensitive ogre. As hard as it is to do, you need to lessen his attachment to you. It's not mean, it's healthy.

Think about it: Is it really necessary to have him sleeping on your lap every second? Does he have to go everywhere you go, all the time? You may love this, but by satisfying your need for affection, you're damaging your dog's mental stability. I know it sucks, but ignore your dog more. If you have one of these dogs, and he sleeps in bed with you, get him a nice comfy dog bed and put him on the floor next to you. It doesn't have to be permanent, only until his separation anxiety has improved.

There are many other behavior issues that plague our dogs, but unfortunately, I don't have the time or space to go through them all here. Most of them are easily manageable once you recognize, and take care of, your dog's canine needs. Every dog out there will have its thing, and you may never be able to totally cure it. However, you can improve the situation, and the sooner you act, the easier it will be to fix, and the happier your life with your dog will be.

8 Crap In, Crap Out

I find that everyone's individual nutrition choices are a very personal thing. Some people will swear by low-carb diets, while others praise the benefits of being a vegetarian, while still others live on frequent liquid detoxes. Once again, everyone is merely doing the best they can with the information at hand, and sometimes that information is inadequate or just plain wrong.

Back before I became a dog trainer, I was a personal trainer and nutritionist for people. I was, and still am, very particular about what I put into my body because I am very aware of what is in the food we eat, and have seen the effects they have on the human body. During the course of my personal training career I tried every kind of diet imaginable and even competed in a natural body building competition (pause for flexing), and one of the things I quickly learned was that if you give your body bad fuel it will run like crap and break down often.

Trying out all of the various diets helped me come to the realization that modern science has really messed us up nutritionally. Human ingenuity has given to the rise and success of fast food restaurants, a plethora of additives and preservatives, and a number of chemical substitutes for real ingredients.

What has all this given us? The rise of obesity, heart disease, osteoporosis, diabetes . . . the list goes on and on. All of the things we've created to give us more convenience and to increase our dietary options are the very things that have directly contributed to leading us to poorer health. However, if you empower yourself with knowledge, it's easy to make the right food choices and live a longer, healthier life.

The pet food industry contains many of the same flaws and obstacles that hamper our own nutritional choices. Every brand of food swears it's the best for your dog, claims to contain all kinds of yummy ingredients, and usually has an irresistibly cute pooch on the bag. The commercials show dogs running to their food bowls, eager to dine on the banquet of colorful shapes which has been set before them. Once finished with the meal, the dogs frolic over to their TV owners to generously thank them for providing such a delicious and nutritious feast. They make it look so good that even I've been tempted to sit down and have a bowl of the stuff (ok, maybe I did, but just that one time).

To add to the confusion, everyone you talk to will recommend something different. The breeder swears by one food, your groomer only uses something else, and the vet advises yet another one. Everyone has their own opinion on dog nutrition; however, very few are actually qualified to be giving out any advice. Before you acccept anyone's recommendation about what to feed your dog, consider two things: 1) does the person have any knowledge as to why the food is good, other than the fact that they feed it to their dog? 2) Does that person have anything to personally gain by you using that particular food (like a vet who only sells that brand of food)?

I'm about to give you my take on canine nutrition and I'll start by telling you I definitely am not an expert. However, because nutrition is so important to me and so important to the well-being of the dogs I work with, I went out and educated myself on the subject (and continue to do so). So although I have some knowledge to share, I encourage you to go out and get more information so that you can make the right nutrition choice for your pack.

I take a very basic approach to nutrition. Forget everything you've ever heard about dog food and let's take a look at what the dog's body is really designed to eat. The first stop is your dog's mouth. Take a look inside and check out all those pointy teeth inside. Notice that you don't see any flat molars in there and that his jaws only open up and down (like a crocodile) and not side to side like ours can. Our jaws move side to side to enable us to chew our food using those flat molars in the back of our mouth. A dog's jaws only open up and down, and their teeth come together like a zipper, perfectly designed for ripping off chunks of food and swallowing them.

Next, we hit the digestive system. Your dog has the identical digestive system of a wolf - not similar but identical. Keep in mind that dogs have only been domesticated for about fifteen thousand years – that's the blink of an eye in evolutionary terms. I know it's hard to believe your little Cocker Spaniel is so closely related to the Gray Wolf, but that's the truth.

All of these observations tell me that dogs are designed to eat what wolves eat. And wolves are pure carnivores eating a diet that is almost exclusively meat. Even that little Chihuahua down the street with the diamond collar and tiara that gets carried around in a Gucci bag, is in essence, a meat-craving carnivore. Like it or not, that's what dogs are made to eat and that's exactly what they need to stay healthy.

Now it's true that during the domestic dog's journey from wild wolf to family pet they have adapted to their environment as needed. To make the transition, dogs quickly became opportunists, eating whatever they could find to survive. That included everything from stale bread, to rotting fruits and vegetables, to bones and anything else available to help them survive from day to day. However, just because they can eat it, doesn't mean they should eat it. I could eat junk food every day and probably survive just fine for quite a while, but not without long term health problems and side effects. The reason that obesity has become such an epidemic in our society is mostly due to the bad food choices that we make for ourselves and our pets.

I personally believe the best diet for dogs is raw meat. Yes, raw. Gasp if you like, but that's what your dog's body is engineered to eat and use. Now you could go to your local butcher and get whole pieces of chicken and beef and supplement it with some added nutrients, but that's a lot of work. I do have a few clients who do it but they are definitely the exception.

The good news is that due to consumer demand, it's getting easier and easier to feed our dogs better food. As people begin to educate themselves and realize how to better take care of their furry family members, they are forcing the pet food industry to adapt. Feeding raw food to your dog used to be left to the hard-core canine purists whom everyone thought were a bit wacky – turns out they were just ahead of their time.

So now you are able to get your pooch raw food without the hassle. Many great companies make completely balanced frozen raw foods that you simply defrost and serve (although most dogs will be more than happy to scoff them down fully frozen). They come in the form of individual patties and medallions, as well as rolls. Although they do contain some fruit and vegetables, most contain about 95% meat.

Raw food diets are especially great for dogs with food allergies, because the ingredients are simple and pure. The problem with many commercial dry foods is that they are packed with things that are necessary for production (to make them crunchy and visually appealing to humans) and preservation (chemicals to preserve the "freshness"), but which are also potentially harmful ingredients to your dog.

The three top food allergens for dogs are wheat, corn and soy. If you pick up any bag of dog food in the supermarket you'll probably find all three lurking there. If they could possibly be harmful to your dog, why would companies put them in there? Why, money, of course. These ingredients are cheap and readily available. The problem with many of the big name dog foods out there is that they spend boat loads of money on advertising and very little on the actual product. Most of these companies are owned by big conglomerates that make just about everything while specializing in nothing. I like dog food companies that make pet food and pet food only. That's all they do, so they want to do it well.

Lucky for us, these big companies can't hide their inadequacies, because they're right there on the label of the product. So, just as I used to advise my human clients, I'm telling you to go out and read labels on dog food, as well. Look at what you're really feeding your dog.

Here's the label from Purina ONE Lamb and Rice Formula Dog Food:

> Lamb (natural source of glucosamine), brewers rice, corn gluten meal, whole grain corn, poultry by-product meal (natural source of glucosamine), oatmeal, animal fat (preserved with mixed tocopherols - a source of vitamin E), lamb meal, animal digest, potassium chloride, calcium carbonate, calcium phosphate, salt, caramel color, L-Lysine monochloride, choline chloride, zinc sulfate, ferrous sulfate, ferrous sulfate, vitamin E supplement, manganese sulfate, niacin, vitamin A supplement, vitamin B12 supplement, pyridoxine hydrochloride, garlic oil, folic acid, vitamin D3 supplement, calcium iodate, biotin, menadione sodium bisulfate complex (source of vitamin K activity), sodium selenite

Now here is the label for Primal Frozen Canine Lamb Formula:

> Lamb, Lamb Hearts, Lamb Livers, Ground Lamb Bones, Organic Kale, Organic Carrots, Organic Yams, Organic Broccoli, Organic Apples, Cranberries, Organic Apple Cider Vinegar, Organic Parsley, Organic Coconut Oil, Organic Kelp, Alfalfa, Salmon Oil, Mixed Tocopherols (source of vitamin E)

I don't know about you, but I'm not too sure what many of the ingredients are that are listed on the Purina bag. I can, however, recognize every single ingredient from the Primal Label. Also, notice the long string of vitamins added to the Purina Dog Food. You may think that's a good thing, but all that means is that the vitamins originally present in their ingredients were completely removed during the production process.

Just reading those two labels is a big wake up call. Simple is better. Natural is better. And don't be fooled just because a company chooses to put the word "natural" in their name. Often, the only thing "natural" about these foods is the word itself.

Okay, let's get back to raw food now. There is one big downside to feeding your dog raw food: it isn't cheap. Just as it's inexpensive to go to Burger King and buy off of their dollar menu, while it's more costly to shop at Whole Foods and buy organic; it's also more expensive to buy raw food for your dog versus those big colorful bags in the supermarket. But always remember: you are what you eat.

Yes, it will cost more to make the switch to raw food initially, but I want you to also consider the money you will save by spending less time at the vet. If you take care of your dog physically and mentally, you will spend far less money on health care.

As you know, when I first decided to make dogs my career, I went to the experts on canine behavior to learn. So when I wanted to learn about nutrition, I did the same thing – only this expert had two legs instead of four.

I took a job at a local holistic pet shop in Bloomfield, New Jersey called Paradise Pet owned by Jeff and Diana Coltenback. Jeff is quite well-known in the local dog community and has helped countless owners find the right nutrition to help their dogs live better and longer. My fingers will cramp up if I try type out all of Jeff's credentials, so I'll sum it up by just saying that he's a canine nutrition guru. I took the job hoping to soak up as much information as I could from him.

While working there, I noticed that about once a month or so, someone would come into the store with a very troubled look on their face and say, "My dog has been diagnosed with this disease, has these conditions and is on these drugs. I've tried everything, nothing seems to help and a friend told me about you." I would watch as Jeff advised them to take their dog off of most or all of their medications, switch foods to raw, and maybe add one or two natural supplements. Nine out of ten times they would be back within a month, smiling, reporting that their dog's health had improved. I quickly became a believer in the power of good nutrition, and a student of Jeff's methods.

That's the impact that eating right can have. Now it can't cure disease or prevent your dog from ever getting ill, but it can improve the symptoms of many serious conditions, as well as keep Fido's body strong and vibrant. Once you try it and see the results, there's no going back.

If you're looking for immediate tangible evidence that a meat-based diet is better for your dog, it's right there in front of you – or, more specifically, below you on the ground (maybe even on the bottom of your shoe). The proof is in the poop. The first thing you'll notice when you make the switch from a grain-heavy diet to raw (or even a meat based dry food) is that your dog will poop about one quarter the amount he used to.

You're feeding your dog the exact same quantity of food but instead of excreting most of it, his body is using it. Poop is merely unnecessary material – what your body can't use, it gets rid of. So instead of all that junk food just wasting time going through your dog's digestive system, you're fueling his body with the nutrients that are needed for optimal health. This is what feeding your dog should be about: giving him the best possible nutrition to ensure that he lives the longest and healthiest life possible. Not just feeding him enough so that he will survive for a given period of time.

Some of the currently popular dry dog foods contain as much as 60-

70% carbohydrates. That's 60–70% of the food that your dog has no use for and just poops out. For me, that's all the proof I need. But for those of you who really enjoy picking up all of that poop, you should stick with that grain-heavy chow.

Raw food is great but it's not for everyone, and it's not the only choice you have out there to better your dog's diet. There is a wide range of choices with raw (in my opinion) at the top and those supermarket foods at the bottom. There are also canned diets, dehydrated foods, granular, home prepared, and a very large selection of good quality dry dog foods. Since I'm trying very hard to keep this book short and sweet, I'm not going to get into every single type of food out there for your dog. However, since the majority of pet owners feed their dogs some kind of dry kibble, I would like to mention that there's a wide selection of grain free dry dog foods that are perfect for people who understand the benefits of a meat based diet but, for whatever reason, don't want to feed raw.

At the moment, you won't find most of these foods in any super pet store or supermarket. For the good stuff, you'll have to seek out a local or holistic pet shop. But times are a-changin'. It won't be long before public demand squeezes out all of the junk foods and ushers in a new wave of dog nutrition choices. It's happening already. Many of the well-known, traditional dog food companies are now offering grain-free selections.

Just know that there are better choices out there, and that you need to educate yourself and find what works best for you and your pack. I think of it this way: I love my dog – a lot - and if feeding her a better, more expensive, higher-quality food means that she'll be with me just one day longer, I'll do it.

Treats and Bones

All the rules that apply to finding good, healthy food apply to treats as well. Just as with your dog's food, all those grains in his snacks aren't doing him any good, either. As a once in a while treat it's not going to harm him, but as a daily addition to his diet it can have an effect. It's kind of like if I have a candy bar today; as long as it's just a rare treat, it shouldn't affect my overall well-being. If I have one candy bar a day though, it won't be long before my body suffers.

I'm sure some of you will tell me that you've had more than a few dogs and you always fed them a typical grain-heavy dry dog food and never had a problem. That doesn't surprise me at all. Dogs can eat just about anything and survive; but do you want your dog to survive, or thrive? Sure, George Burns smoked cigars every day of his adult life and still managed to live to 100, but that doesn't mean smoking is the right thing to do if you want to be healthy. For every George Burns there are hundreds of people who die from the exact same poor health habits.

So stick to meat-based treats and read the ingredients on the label. Don't be fooled by packaging or appearance either. Companies are very good at making junk food look like real meat so always read the labels. Try to always purchase products which are made here in the United States where we have much higher production and manufacturing standards.

Bones are a great supplement to any dog's diet. They can satisfy Fido's desire to chew, help clean his teeth, and provide some additional nutrition. Just make sure the bones are raw and not cooked. NEVER give your dog a cooked bone. Cooked bones can splinter and rip up your dog's insides, so if you want to indulge him in a bone, make it raw. They can be frozen or defrosted, but never cooked, steamed, broiled or baked.

Are there any dog owners left out there that don't know that rawhide is bad for your pooch? I guess there are because I still see it being sold, so here's the deal on rawhide. Rawhide is simply the hide of a cow - basically leather before the tanning process. The biggest threat with rawhide is that it can cause an obstruction in the intestinal tract. Just picture what wet rawhide looks like – like a big wad of chewed gum. Now imagine continually swallowing large pieces of it. It's easy to imagine how it can cause a blockage inside your poor dog's stomach.

So if you have rawhide in your house at this moment, I want you put down this book, go get it, throw it away and then pat yourself on the back – you just made your dog healthier. There are plenty of other great product choices to satisfy your dog's need to chew. Bully sticks, pig's ears, beef tendons and trachea are just a few of the all-natural ways to give Rover his chewing fix.

There's much more to learn about dog nutrition, but that's all you're getting from me at this time. Take this taste of information and go out and learn as much as your inquisitive heart desires. Just make sure you start to really think about what you're putting inside your dog, and find the right choices for you and your dog.

At this time you may have to go a little out of your way to find the best food choice for your furry best friend but isn't he worth it? It won't be long before you can find really high-quality food everywhere. I predict that within the next five to ten years there will be freezers of raw dog food in every pet shop and rawhide bones will finally be extinct. I already see bully sticks replacing rawhide and grain-free foods moving their way up the pet store shelves. The pet industry is changing almost daily as we learn how to take better care of our dogs, and by refusing to settle for anything that might not be in our dogs' best interest.

Misguided Advice

Get ready, I'm about to pick on vets (at ease, I'm talking about veterinarians not war veterans). And I'm not picking on all vets, just some vets. Remember, we are only now truly learning what it means to take proper physical and mental care of our dogs. Just as the pet food industry is rapidly changing, so too is the pet medical industry. We're learning now that many vaccines don't need to be given yearly and some may not be necessary at all. We're learning the value of early socialization BEFORE all of the puppy shots have been completed (more on this in the next chapter). Veterinarians need to keep up with new information and be open minded to change and recognize that there are some topics that they may not be adequately qualified to address.

There are two subjects that I find most traditional vets are not properly equipped to handle, and they are nutrition and behavior. The reason is that they're not trained appropriately in these two areas. It's not their fault; it's just not what they are trained to deal with. The problem with some vets is that although they are not really trained in behavior and nutrition, it doesn't stop them from giving out generous portions of bad advice. Not all vets, but some.

I've had to undo a lot of damage that was created by bad advice delivered by vets. More than a few times, I've stared in disbelief as a client describes what the vet instructed him to do to his dog. I don't blame vets for not knowing, I blame them for so freely advising on topics in which they have no experience.

If you tell the average traditional vet you're feeding your dog raw food he's going to go nuts, saying how bad it is for him and that the bacteria will harm him and it will ruin his teeth, and so on. If we were talking about a human I would agree, but not a dog, not a carnivore, and not an animal so evolutionary similar to the wolf.

Not all vets, but some. Have I said that yet? Good, well it needs repeating because I can see the hate mail from vets coming in already. Don't get me wrong, I am very much pro-vet. If your dog is sick or injured take him immediately to the vet. However, if you have a behavioral problem, call a dog behavior specialist. If you need nutrition advice, find someone who is well-educated in canine nutrition.

Ultimately, you have to do what you feel is best for your dog. If you've gone out and empowered yourself with knowledge, you can't go wrong. No matter how sure you are that what you're doing is the right choice, keep that mind open because you never know when better information will make itself available.

9 Early Intervention

Approximately 70% of dogs in animal shelters are there due to behavioral issues. Of those dogs unlucky enough to land there, 60% of them will be euthanized. That's an awful lot of dogs sentenced to death each year. Why are these dogs plagued with so many behavior problems? In a word, us. We are to blame, we help shape these bad behaviors (both voluntarily and involuntarily), and then abandon our dogs when they need us most.

What gets me so fired up is that it's so easily avoidable if people would just pull their heads out of the sand and learn what it takes to take care of a dog. When you get a dog, you're not getting a possession that you can simply discard if it "doesn't work out," you're taking in another living thing with the understanding that you MUST do everything in your power to ensure that the dog is with you his entire life. Not until you get tired of taking care of it, not unless it pees in the house, not unless it gets in the way of your social calendar – for life, no exceptions.

I'm sure everyone that brings home a new puppy says that they're going to have them forever and ever and take such good care of them, but the cold hard truth is that 25% of people will give up their dog before it's a year old. One out of four! And the reason is almost always behavior issues – issues that we created by not doing the right things early on, and issues that we ignored, assuming they would just magically get better.

My job is to make sure that you're not part of that 25%, and that your dog is given the life he deserves. If I'm coming across a little too gloom and doom, good. I'm trying to make a big enough noise so that you will take some initiative and do the right thing for your dog. I sound serious because this is a very serious situation that is so easily prevented. All you have to do is gain a little knowledge, and put in some time and effort when your dog is a puppy.

The beginning of a dog's life is, without question, the most important time of his life. It's during this time that they are little sponges, soaking up all the experiences they can find. I plan on putting together a complete book on raising a well-balanced puppy sometime in the future, but I feel this is too important a topic to wait. I see too many uniformed people neglecting to take the simple, necessary steps to ensure that they'll never consider giving up their dog.

In this book I'm only going to touch on the basic, most important aspect of helping a puppy develop into a fine well-adjusted adult dog, but nothing more. I highly recommend that anyone who has a new puppy, will be getting a new puppy, or is even considering a puppy get informed somehow (read some articles or books or hire a good trainer) so you can start your puppy's life off the right way.

For now, I'm only going to spend time on one word and one word only. This one word is the most important thing you should be doing with your puppy and should take precedence over everything else. I want you to make little signs with this word on it and stick them all over your home and office. I want you to change the lyrics to all of your favorite songs to include this word. I want you to wake up each morning and shout out this word as you swing your legs off the bed and onto the floor. Most importantly, I want you to live this word with your puppy every single day.

The magical word is . . . (drum roll) . . . socialization. Yes, socialization, damn it! Not socialization the way you think of it, socialization the way it's supposed to be done. I can't believe what some people call socializing their dog. Very few people seem to get this right and it is without a doubt the one thing that can make all the difference.

Hopefully, I've convinced you just how important socialization is, so now let's get on to the why's, what's and how's of it. True socialization is getting your dog accustomed to and confident around everything in this crazy world. I want your dog to have a "been there done that" attitude by the time he's six months of age.

Many people make the mistake of only exposing their puppy to things in their present day-to-day life, but you need to think outside the box here. I don't care if you don't own a cat, find one and let your pup learn how to behave around it. That way, when your daughter comes home from college with one piece of luggage that's meowing you will have a much better chance of everyone getting along.

The three things I want you to concentrate on are socialization to people, dogs and environments. Those three will impact just about every puppy's (and owner's) life and those are three things that need to be addressed in mass quantities.

So, what do you consider adequate socialization for you puppy? Let's start with people. How many people would you say is good? Forget it, don't even guess – I guarantee its way under what is required. I recently attended a seminar by Dr. Ian Dunbar, who is considered by most dog behavior professionals to be the foremost authority on puppies (and dog behavior in general). He believes that every puppy should have contact with 100 different people by the time he's eight weeks old (that means you, breeders) and another 100 during the next eight weeks. In case you're keeping score at home that's 200 different people your dog should have interacted with by the time it hits four months of age.

So is there anyone out there who can really say that they properly socialized their puppies to people? I didn't think so. Although I agree with Dr. Dunbar, I'm also a realist and know that no one on the planet is going to come close to those numbers. So, for my puppy classes, everyone's homework is to have their puppies meet at least ten new people and dogs every week. I would feel much better if it was ten a day, but I understand that most of you can't quit your jobs to socialize your dog.

There really is no magic number here, but more is without a doubt better. Your dog also needs to meet all different kinds of people. Every race and ethnic group, tall, short, fat, skinny, old, young, babies, people wearing glasses and hats, people carrying umbrellas, people on crutches and using canes and in wheel chairs, people wearing Halloween costumes, Santa, people in winter coats and wearing brightly colored rain jackets, people on roller skates and scooters and skate boards, people, people, people.

Let all of these people interact with and handle your puppy, but supervise everything. It's very important that all of these encounters be positive experiences for your pup or else we'll be headed in the wrong direction in a hurry. Most puppies will be more than thrilled at the attention, but keep a close watch on your dog's body language and recognize when you should give him a reprieve from of all those reaching hands.

Be especially careful during interactions with children, as children can tend to get overcome with the cuteness of puppies, and their innocent enthusiasm can lead to aggressive groping that can cause your puppy to become leery with children. I never recommend a puppy for someone with very young children who can't yet understand that there are rules to playing with a puppy. If you've got young children you've already got a puppy – the human kind – so you're attention will undoubtedly be divided, and ultimately, the dog will be neglected.

All of the above guidelines also apply to socialization with dogs. Letting your dog sniff three butts a week during your walks around the block will just not cut it. You should also be aware that true dog interaction is without human constraints, meaning without being tethered to you by a leash. Puppies must be allowed to interact with other dogs in an off-leash environment so that they can learn bite inhibition.

Bite inhibition is basically your pup learning that those pointy teeth he has inside his mouth hurt. If you watch two well-socialized adult dogs playing, you'll notice that they're constantly mouthing each other yet never hurt each other with all those teeth. When they were puppies they did the same endless mouthing, but every once in a while they would bite a little too hard and the other dog would yelp, and both dogs would stop playing and look at each other. The dog that chomped down a little too hard would realize that if he wants to keep playing – and he does – he has to pull his punches.

That's exactly why those puppy teeth are like little pointy needles– to enable the pup to learn that biting hurts and give him a nice soft mouth. Most puppies will put up with an awful lot of inappropriate biting, so it's important that you socialize your pup with older dogs as well. Older dogs will not tolerate too much juvenile behavior and will make corrections accordingly. By letting your pup interact with older dogs he will learn that not every dog enjoys being treated like a squeaky toy.

So I'm begging you to go out there and socialize your dog as soon as you bring his furry little body home. This is another situation that will get you into big trouble if you listen to your vet (oh boy, here I go again). The standard protocol for vets (you know the deal, some vets – not all) is to tell a new puppy owner not to let his pup around any other dogs until all of his vaccinations are complete (which could be as long as six months). One client of mine had a vet tell them that they shouldn't even let him leave the house, which is just pure insanity.

He tells you this because he's worried about diseases like Parvo (Canine Parvovirus), which can be life-threatening to your puppy. The problem is that if you wait to socialize your dog until after all of his vaccines are complete, there's a good chance you're giving him a death sentence. At six months of age, most of the prime socialization period is behind him and you may be in for a very long haul until he becomes comfortable around his canine brethren.

Now don't get me wrong, I understand where your vet is coming from. His job is to preserve the physical health of your dog as best he can. The problem with avoiding contact with other dogs is that he's doing that at the cost of your dog's mental health, which is just as important.

We can do both though. I don't want you to take your new pup to the dog park where we know nothing about the health of the other dogs. Instead, set up encounters with other dogs you know are healthy and have all of the proper vaccinations. Play dates with people you know are a great way to get together with friends while getting your puppy the quality canine time he desperately needs. Doggie daycares are perfect for socialization providing they will take a young pup (not all do). There, he'll play with ten to twenty dogs in one day in a clean, safe environment.

So please, let your puppy play with as many dogs as possible, but be smart about it. If you don't create these kinds of encounters for your new pup early on you may be on your way to creating an adult dog that is fearful, anxious and/or aggressive with other dogs.

The next stop on our journey of socialization enlightenment is environment. The human world is filled with all kinds of weird places, noises, contraptions and events, and unless your pooch learns about these things as a puppy, there's a possibility that he may really freak out when exposed to them when he's older. However, if he's seen it all when he's young, he will learn that all this weird stuff in the human world is not going to harm him.

It's like if you woke up this morning and a UFO was parked in your back yard. I'm pretty sure it would make you more than a little uneasy (a change of underwear may even be in order). But if you've seen some UFO's before and nothing bad happened, you would probably be okay with it.

Everything your dog sees for the first time is a UFO to him. If, by a year old, your dog has never seen a moving train, and one goes by making all that noise, he's going to go into panic mode. Think about how scary an experience it would be if you weren't expecting it and had no idea what it was. So we need to get your dog exposed to everything possible that this human world of ours has to throw at him. That way, no matter where your life takes you and your dog, he will be cool with it. Even if you live nowhere near a train and have no plans of ever being around one, you must find one and let your puppy experience it. You never know where life will take you, but if you make a concerted effort to expose your dog to as much as possible, you can be confident that he'll adapt easily.

Start with things that are in your everyday life and then move on to the more unusual and obscure. Begin in your home with every appliance and gadget you own: dishwashers, coffee makers, hair dryers, garbage cans, cameras, fans, umbrellas and anything and everything else you can think of. Then, hit the road and show your puppy the world: the bank, the groomer, fireworks, cars, trucks, busses, planes, rivers, the ocean, bicycles, skateboards, rollerblades, scooters, parades, concerts, big cities, large crowds, subways and whatever else you can expose him to.

One point to remember is that we need all of these experiences to be either positive or a non-event. It's natural for your dog to be nervous or unsure around something he's never seen before, but we need to keep him around it until he sees that although it may look scary and make loud noises, it's not going to harm him. Be careful not to overwhelm your pup, and recognize when a situation may be too much stimulation for him, or at too high an intensity. For something like a train, for example, you should start a good distance away from the tracks, and then slowly move closer as your dog adjusts. As his leader and protector it's up to you to help communicate that these experiences are no big deal, and how you act in these situations is crucial to your dog's development. That means that you cannot do what your human nature is going to tell you to do.

Your dog is always looking to you for support and leadership and he's constantly reading your body language and energy to gauge how he should feel. If your puppy shows any signs of anxiety or nervousness, or becomes fearful as you are exposing him to things, DO NOT coddle him and tell him "everything is okay." If you do, you're amplifying his unstable state of mind. Remember, every time you give your dog affection you are reinforcing what he's doing at that exact moment as well as his state of mind at that exact moment.

Let's use thunder as an example, since many dogs develop phobias to thunder and lightning storms. You're sitting at home and thunder booms above you so loud that the whole house seems to shake. Your puppy understandably gets scared, drops his head and tail, and moves over to you, shaking. The human in you will want to pick the little guy up and assure him that everything is going to be alright. But if you do, you'll be giving affection to an unstable mind, and so the next time your puppy is presented with the same circumstances, he will immediately go back to the state of mind where the affection was given.

What he needs in that situation is a stable, confident leader. You need to halt the human desire to reassure your pup, and think like a dog and be that leader. If thunder booms overhead, scaring your puppy, he will be looking to you for support and to show him whether he should be afraid. If you ignore the thunder and your dog's reaction, and pretend like nothing's wrong (because there is nothing wrong) your dog will think, "Wow, that was scary. But my leader's okay with it and nothing bad happened to me. Oh well, I guess it's no big deal."

Now, if your dog is so scared that he's wetting the floor and having a total melt-down, we need to take him away from the stimulus and work with him at a comfortable distance and intensity. If it's a train that has him spooked, move away from it until you notice that he's slightly uneasy but not shutting down. This is where you will want to spend some time and let him become acclimated to being around the train and having nothing bad happen. You can redirect him with a game or treats to give his mind something else to focus on, or you can just hang out there for a while and let him settle down.

Once a fear or anxiety has been established, it's very important not to push your puppy too far too fast. You always have to proceed at his pace, not yours. Watch your dog's body language and recognize when he's had enough for the day. Try to keep exposures brief, but repeat them over time. A good guide for a food-motivated dog is that if he will take a treat, he's not that scared. If he won't, then the distance or intensity is too much for him, and we need to take it back and down a notch.

There's so much that goes into raising a happy, healthy puppy, and if you don't take full advantage of this early impressionable time in their lives you could be in for some big problems in the future. Don't assume that little issues will just get better over time. Address them as they come up so you can treat them quickly and easily. I think everyone can benefit from a private session with a professional or a good puppy kindergarten class. The small cost now could be the difference between having a long, happy life with a well-balanced pooch, and being forced to abandon a troubled dog. I guarantee you're dog will pay you back tenfold in love.

10 A Dog's Life

Our relationship with the domestic dog has evolved greatly in the limited time that we've been together. It really wasn't that long ago that the dog was nothing more than a possession that was kept outside in a dog house and simply fed whatever scraps were left over. Now, however, we've invited dogs into our homes, families and hearts, and we are treating them with the love and care that we give our own children. We are going out of our way to truly understand our dog's needs and what it really means to take care of them properly.

A dog house is not good enough. A rolled up newspaper as discipline is unacceptable. Having a dog that jumps on visitors or that chews us out of house and home is no longer tolerated. We are finally realizing that our dogs can live better in our world and we can enjoy them more. Troublesome behaviors can be treated and addressed.

Old dogs can be taught new tricks and dogs of any age can change - but only if we change first.

It all starts with that nice open mind I mention so often, and by empowering yourself with knowledge. If there's anything you want to change about your dog, or if you just want to see how you can enhance your relationship with him further, do something about it. There are plenty of resources out there to help you with your dog; you've just got to go out and get them. If you want something to change, you have to change something. How can you expect things to just magically get better by sitting back and doing nothing?

I can't stand it when people see me with my dog and say, "You're so lucky. You have such a good dog." Luck has nothing to do with it. I created the relationship I have with my dog and took the time to work with her every single day to teach her the rules of my pack and live happily in the human world. That kind of relationship and that kind of dog is yours, too – provided you learn what it takes and spend the necessary time with your dog.

Unfortunately, we live in a world in which everyone expects instant gratification. We have no patience to wait for anything, and fast is never fast enough. Training your dog takes time, as does building a solid relationship with him. Some things, like leadership, can have an immediate effect, but most of the time training your dog is a numbers game. It takes constant repetition and consistency. The more time you spend with your dog, the quicker the process will be.

Don't forget that every dog and every person is different. What might take one person a short period of time to accomplish with their dog may take a bit longer with your pooch. Never compare your dog or your relationship with your dog to another dog and his handler. Instead, concentrate on your own dog and make sure your relationship is always improving. Everyone will be progressing at their own pace and having different successes, and experiencing individual setbacks, as well.

Every person, family and pack will have a different set of rules and will expect different things from their dogs. It doesn't matter what I expect of my dog or what your neighbor does or what rules your brother has with his pooch. You do what works best for you and your pack. I recommend everyone call a family meeting and decide together what the rules of the house are for your dog. Is jumping acceptable? Is he allowed on the furniture? Can he sleep in bed with you? Everything needs to be agreed upon by everyone and you must be united in the training. If one person out of five lets him on the couch, he'll do it just about every time. If you're not consistent, Rover will get a lot of mixed signals and never fully understand the rules. There really is no right or wrong rule, as long as everything is done on your terms and not on your dogs' terms.

A big mistake I made way back before I became empowered with knowledge is that I expected my dog to be perfect. I now realize how unrealistic that is, and how incredibly unfair that was to my dog. Dogs will always be dogs and will always behave like dogs. If your dog smells or hears an animal outside your house, he's going to react because that's what dogs do. The thing you can work on is how fast you can get him back from the reaction.

Training takes time, but if you recognize this fact and celebrate the little improvements along the way, you can enjoy the process and strengthen your bond with your furry pal. Always remember that whatever issues you're working on, you must go at the dog's pace, not yours. Stock up on patience and never give up on your dog. After all the dopey things we've done to our dogs over the years, they never seem to give up on us.

Think Like a Dog

This book is designed to help you improve your life with your dog and I've gone over many ways that you can help your dog become a more balanced and happy member of your family. But never forget that relationships are a two-way street. If you just open yourself up, your dog can teach you how to become a well-balanced and happier person too.

The human world comes with a long list of obligations, responsibilities and challenges; however, it also has so much joy, love and happiness. Unfortunately, we have a tendency to fixate on the stresses of life and overlook the simple pleasures in our daily lives. We go through life regretting past failures and preparing for future hurdles without taking the time to enjoy the little things all around us.

Here's where we really need to let our dogs open our eyes to a new way of living. Dogs live in the present moment with no regard for what's going to happen down the road, and they waste no time dwelling on the past. They care only about what's happening right now at this exact moment. Buddhist Monks call it "mindfulness", and it is the key to the canine existence.

Not only do dogs care exclusively about what's happening at this exact moment but they also take great joy in very simple, common place events. The next time you're on your way out the door to take your dog for a walk, take a good look at him. He's probably elated. Even though this could be his third walk of the day, twenty-first walk of the week and one-thousandth walk of the year, he's totally over-joyed. If you pick up a toy to play with your dog he looks like he just won the lottery.

Why do these same repetitive daily routines make our dogs so happy? It makes them happy because they let it. It's that simple. They open themselves up to the experience as if there was nothing else in world to be doing at that time. While you're on your usual ten minute walk around the block (hopefully that will be much longer now), your dog isn't thinking about the other things you could be doing, or how long he's going to have to wait for the next walk. He's enjoying every single step he takes on this walk.

We have the power to do the same thing, but it takes a bit more con-scious effort and will power. You really have to train your mind to put aside your human inclinations to think about everything going on in your life and experience what's right in front of you. Every time you're with your dog I want you to say to yourself, "Think like a dog." Really put your whole mind and body into the time you're sharing with your dog and have fun. All your stresses and worries will be right there waiting for you when you're done.

Life for a dog is fun, and life with a dog is supposed to be too. Every-thing you do with your dog can be enjoyable for both you and Fido. If it's done correctly, leadership, training, and discipline should be pleasurable. Yes, there are times when you need to be firm and seri-ous, but once your message is received and the moment is over, it's back to having fun again. Dogs love fun, and if you can make training fun, they'll be more than willing to comply.

Also, be careful not to concentrate only on bad behaviors, because if you really think about it, most dogs are good much more than they are causing trouble. Some people are quick to correct bad behaviors but forget to praise all of the simple, good stuff. If your dog is not mounting the mailman, dining on your new shoes, or chasing the neighborhood kids up a tree, tell him. Praise him, pet him, play with him or anything else that will send him the message that this is behavior that you like and want more of.

Without fail, my dog makes me smile every single day we're together. Whether it's the way she sleeps upside down with her legs in the air, or how she walks over to a chair and places her head on it, waiting for me to notice how cute she looks, or the way she tolerates the constant probing and poking from my daughters. Our dogs have the ability to brighten our lives on a daily basis, and I strongly believe it's our obligation to return the favor.

Unfortunately, in the grand scheme of life, the time we get with our dogs is so terribly fleeting. Every day with our dogs is a gift for us to cherish or squander. Their life span is way too short compared to ours, and I, for one, intend to celebrate every single day that I get to share with my furry best friend.

Every single night before I turn in, I make one last stop at my dog's bed. I lie down beside her, give her a single kiss on the ear, and thank her. I thank her for abandoning her life in the wild to live with me, a mere human. I thank her for adopting me even though I have behavior problems and am often unstable. I thank her for accepting my strange rules and requirements, like sitting when she's not really tired and being calm when visitors come instead of giving them the exuberant welcome they deserve. Mostly, I thank her for doing what she does best, being a dog. I've always felt that every day with a dog is a good day. Enjoy yours.

Recommended Reading

Hungry for more knowledge? Here are some of my favorite books on dog behavior.

Canine Body Language – A Photographic Guide
Brenda Aloff

How to Speak Dog
Stanley Coren

The Dog's Mind
Bruce Fogle

The Other End of the Leash,
Patricia McConnell

Cesar's Way
Cesar Millan

Also, check out Ian Dunbar's website for training and behavior tips and information:
www.dogstardaily.com

Also by Fernando Camacho

Natural disasters ravage the world, while people scramble to save themselves. On the day the terror strikes New Jersey, Ryan finds a strange dog on his doorstep. The dog looks like an average stray, but Ryan soon learns that this is no ordinary canine. Guided by this extraordinary dog, Ryan travels across the countryside, surviving everything from raging fires to explosive earthquakes. Along the way, he is joined by other survivors and together they are witness to the evils and injustices of man. To stay alive, Ryan must not only put his faith in this unique dog, but in himself as well. Soon, Ryan realizes that he's not only fighting for his own survival, but the survival of all mankind.

Available at www.amazon.com.